Meadowood
Anthology

1905-2011

Meadowood
Anthology
1905-2011

Memories in Miniature

An anthology edited by
Barbara Restle

authorHOUSE®

AuthorHouse™
1663 Liberty Drive
Bloomington, IN 47403
www.authorhouse.com
Phone: 1-800-839-8640

Published by AuthorHouse   06/09/2012

ISBN: 978-1-4772-1185-4 (sc)
ISBN: 978-1-4772-1186-1 (e)

Library of Congress Control Number: 2012909500

Any people depicted in stock imagery provided by Thinkstock are models,
and such images are being used for illustrative purposes only.
Certain stock imagery © Thinkstock.

This book is printed on acid-free paper.

Introduction

In 2005 Ledford Carter established the MEADOWOOD ANTHOLOGY, a quarterly publication for and by the residents of the Bloomington Meadowood Retirement Community. Ledford and his wife Julia have lived in Meadowood for 29 years. His vision was for residents to share and link their life journeys together with their memoirs and poems. Ledford appointed a committee to choose and edit all submissions and although members of this pro-bono group changed during six years of publication, the enthusiasm for this project has never diminished. Many residents were delighted to see their stories in print and the committee soon felt confident that the anthology would survive many more publications. Occasionally members of the committee knew of residents who had interesting experiences to share and urged them to put pen to paper.

Most of the residents have connections to Indiana University. We have many retired professors with "distinguished professor emeritus" awards who are internationally known in their academic fields. We have residents who graduated from this university many years ago and somehow could not tear themselves away from Bloomington. Many of our residents retired from some other workplace in the world, and as we charmingly remind ourselves, returned to Bloomington, to "Age in Place" and to go "Home". For many it has been a dream that came true.

We have memoirs of Jewish residents who escaped Germany and Austria during WW II. One of our Jewish ladies living here survived the Lodz Ghetto Camp in Poland. An author who had been an Italian Resistance Fighter in northern Italy and imprisoned by the Germans submitted a story with a surprising touch of humor.

Some of the more poignant stories are from the wives of WW II American military personnel, who managed to stay in close touch with their husbands while maintaining that "new-normal" family life back home. A few wives were able to follow their husbands to American bases in the United States and the Philippines, while most of the wives were not able to see their husbands for several years. The women coped with humor and good cheer and many went to work on some level for the war effort.

The stories reflect multigenerational memories. One author writes about her parent's reaction to seeing neighbors going without food during the Great Depression and remembers her Mother slipping cardboard inside worn-out shoes. We have stories by men and women who had experienced service in three wars: WWII, the Korean War, and Vietnam War. One resident submitted an on-sight report of witnessing the beginning of Arab Spring. Some of the authors avoid the grimness of their experiences and write with a sense of the ridiculous. One night when food was scarce, soldiers were hungry, they managed to purloin and cook the pigeoneer's birds that he had trained for two years to carry messages between war zones.

Aging in place, has not created a vacuum in intellectual or charitable activities. We have one retired political science professor who creates the monthly lecture series of visiting world famous men and women who guide international policy. And in contrast we have one resident who claims not having read a book in 20 years. However, he is well known for his daily trips, through good or severe weather, by delivering Meals-On-Wheels to home-bound elderly. And this is also the man, who before retiring was a driving force at NASA.

We have an eclectic assemblage of residents who have also learned through their journey in life, that there is no need, during our many social hours, to subordinate themselves in dialogue with another.

Ultimately the memoirs in the Meadowood Anthology give us stories of the common place and also of remarkable events in the lives of possibly one of the greatest generations in American history.

Barbara Restle

Acknowledgements

Without Professor Ledford Carter's ardent enthusiasm for creating the MEADOWOOD ANTHOLOGY this publication would never have seen light. Ledford was successful in requesting funding for the project from members of the Meadowood Memorial Board, which included Attorney Tom McGlassen, Treasurer Phillipa Guthrie and Lesa Huber. Without their loyal and enthusiastic support, this four times a year publication could not have been published.

For the five years I served on the committee of this publication and eventually also worked as the first project manager. I am sincerely grateful to all the members for their hard work and many hours of lively discussions on submitted stories. In the first year this was an arduous decision-making time, however, we were committed to every issue being the best. Therefore, I want to thank each member individually: Jan Skinner, Virginia Gest, Ed deJean, Beth Van Vorst Gray, Ella Fox, Henry Gray, Gene Merrell and Miriam Rosenzweig. We were very fortunate to have our first salaried production editor to be the Herald Times reporter, Leora Baude. Sandie Alexandra Lynch is at this time our talented and patient production editor and consultant.

Without the competent assistance of Meadowood's Receptionist Susan Zurface, many of our earlier submitted manuscripts would have disappeared into Meadowood's nether land. I am also grateful to Jerry McIntosh who stepped in at a crucial time in the electronic proof reading of the manuscript, saving me many hours at the computer.

Barbara Restle

Table of Contents

PART I: MEMOIRS IN MINIATURE

PART II: MEMORIES OF WARS

PART III: POEMS

PART I

MEMOIRS IN MINIATURE

A MAN'S REAL POSSESSION IS HIS MEMORY

IN NOTHING ELSE IS HE RICH

IN NOTHING ELSE IS HE POOR

By Alexander Smith

(1830-1867)

THE PLAIN MAN IS THE BASIC CLOD

FROM WHICH WE GROW THE DEMIGOD

AND IN THE AVERAGE MAN IS CURLED

THE HERO STUFF THAT RULES THE WORLD

By Sam Walters Foss

(1858-1911)

The "Luck" of Herman Wells

By Howard Gest

In 1966 I came to I.U. as chairman of the Department of Microbiology. In this capacity, I had several kinds of interactions with Dr. Herman B. Wells and quickly realized why he had such a legendary reputation. Example: Many years ago, while walking in Greenwich, England, one day at about 1 p.m., I ran into Dr. Wells unexpectedly. He was just leaving, and on his way to Paris. I asked him to recommend an eating place. At least eight months later, I passed him on campus, and he immediately asked me how I had enjoyed the lunch.

Over the course of many years, we often had sequential appointments at the small shop of "retired" barber John Plew, who had managed the I.U. Memorial Union Barber Shop. This afforded opportunities for chit-chat and reminiscences. As Wells approached his 85th birthday, I decided to give him a small personal gift: namely, a specially printed and framed quotation from Cicero's famous essay "On Old Age." Here is the excerpt I chose:

> "So people who declare that there are no activities for old age are speaking beside the point. It is like saying that the pilot has nothing to do with sailing as ship because he leaves others to climb the masts and run along the gangways and work the pumps, while he himself sits quietly in the stern holding the rudder. He may not be doing what the younger men are doing, but his contribution is much more significant and valuable than theirs. Great deeds are not done by strength or speed or physique; they are the products of thought, and character, and judgment. And far from diminishing, such qualities actually increase with age.

Recently, in shuffling through some treasures I had saved, I came across Dr. Wells' acknowledgement dated July 24, 1987:

> Dear Howard: You're proving that your memory is just as good as ever. I appreciate the pages from Cicero's essay and the paragraph which you are using is indeed a good choice. I note that Cicero was 62 at the time he was speaking these brave words about Cato at 84, and I'm inclined to accept

them. However, I think it's worth noting the difference between 62 and 85 or 86 is considerable.

We will indeed get the entire essay, and I'm sure to enjoy it thoroughly. Thank you for remembering. With warm good wishes, I am Sincerely, Herman

Herman Wells' autobiography was titled "Being Lucky." Yes, being lucky helps, but Wells had unique gifts that built an academic institution that reached around the world. He was a man of great character. ⁂

Letter to My Old Friends in Georgetown

By Alfred Boissevain

Greetings from a different world! I loved the
last
as well as the several before them. And I love
this one.
Most of the people here are old, and I
qualify
in that respect. They have all been closely
related to
Indiana University; usually as professors on a
limitless variety of subjects. I wish, however,
I could join in when they all show their
unbounded exuberance for football and
basketball.
A special factor here is the School of Music
at IU.
There are, for instance, three full student
orchestras
presenting a steady stream of programs at
the
concert hall on campus. We have a bus and
driver;
and no charges for the chauffeuring either.
The food here is plentiful and excellent, but
is secondary
to the fact that Claire, my daughter lives only
a brief mile away.
Regarding the weather; enough said. My
salvation is my
ability to close my eyes and visualize the
California Sierra summit
while the dawn approaches, slowly dimming
the constellation of stars.

In Remembrance of George Keller, 1917-2005

By Bernard Clayton, Jr.

Author's note: George Keller was a neighbor and a friend. Several years ago I wrote this in my journal about this remarkable man.

When George moves from here to there in the Meadowood dining room, he doesn't walk or stride or shuffle: He strolls. It is a stroll not simply to enter or exit the room gracefully (which it does), but a stroll with a purpose. He is the picture of joie de vivre, of well being, of a happy man. He casts the feeling that all is well with the world.

He strolls the room. A touch on a lady's shoulder here to ask about her health, or a touch on the shoulder there to remind one of a concert later in the evening, or a gentle word to a young waitress (three days on the job) who just spilled a second cup of coffee.

If someone from some other place, for the first time, watched George talking or strolling, they could well assume that this place is his. In a way it is. The mood among the diners is always more upbeat when George is there. An aura of gentility surrounds him whether strolling down a corridor or strolling to catch the bus.

George bespeaks good cheer. He never met a downside of life he didn't see its upside. A treasured tree blows down in a fierce storm. George sees the good side. "It will improve the view of the meadow on the other side, and besides, look at all the cord wood for the fireplace next winter." Or when he speaks to an ill patient in the health pavilion: "My, you look good today," and holds her hand.

George does everything with spirited self-confidence and panache. One among the many things he has done in a lifetime filled with achievements is work as a circus ringmaster—20 years with Windjammers Unlimited Concert Circus Band. His closets are filled with attire not only for ring mastering but also for a wide range of roles. Whatever he is costumed for, on him it is natural and perfect. George was born to wear those banners, uniforms, hats and robes, which on me would look outlandish. On George, they are always just right for the occasion.

George would have no qualms strolling toward Queen Elizabeth seated on her throne to be knighted. It would be exactly as George figured it would be. He would fit in perfectly—no qualms.

But that was only one level, one facet of this man's rich and rewarding life. There was an even deeper thrust in his work with veteran's groups and with his church and in his warm relationships with patients in our health pavilion.

I will miss his "hi, neighbor."

*✱

Bernard Clayton, Jr., was a war correspondent for Time-Life Magazines in the Pacific theater for most of World War II. He is best known as the author of several best-selling cookbooks.

An Adventure in Iran

By Jim Weigand

In 1976, I went to Iran to be part of an international conference and to teach at the University of Isfahan, Iran. During that period, an agreement was reached between the American School of Isfahan and Indiana University. During 1977 and 1978, Indiana University sent faculty to teach in Isfahan. The program was a success until late 1978. Our fall faculty member was Mike Chiapetta (now a fellow Meadowood resident). He returned to IU in October of that year, and I was the next faculty member to teach in the program.

I was with my wife in Athens, Greece. There I checked with the embassy to see if travel to Iran would be safe given recent problems with the Shah of Iran, and was told that there would be no problem. I kissed my wife goodbye, and flew to Teheran.

As we were flying over Iraq, we were notified that riots were occurring in the streets of Teheran and the city was ablaze with numerous fires. I was further notified that the plane would continue to Iran, and passengers would be given additional information upon landing, as we neared Teheran's Mehrabad airport. The city below was indeed in flames.

After landing, we were told the city was under a 9:00 p.m. curfew, but we would get a pass to get to a safe location. I called friends at the Teheran American School and was instructed to secure a taxi to transport me to the school, and to knock at the iron gate when I arrived.

I secured a taxi; and the driver's name was Majek, which I changed later to "Magic". He was wonderful. As we went through the city streets he pointed out each fire by saying "bank", "cinema", "liquor". All the fires were at Rockefeller-controlled banks, western cinemas, and liquor stores. These were all businesses that the Shah had westernized, and were despised by the Shiite Muslims.

At many checkpoints, a soldier would aim his rifle at me while the officer checked my pass. This stopping of the taxi occurred about six or seven times. About two hours later leaving the airport, we arrived at the Teheran American School. I stayed at the school for two days, and realized I should try to get to Isfahan. On that early morning, I boarded a bus for the seven-hour trip to Isfahan. The first stop was Qom, home of Ayatollah Khomeini. The streets were filled with protesters carrying anti-American posters, and I was fearful that I could be harmed, so I purchased sugar candies, similar to pralines, and handed them to children with a smile on my face. I thought to myself that no one would harm someone who gave candy to children. Eventually, I arrived in Isfahan with no further difficulties.

After being settled in Isfahan, I began teaching under very stressful conditions. We would start class at 9:00 a.m. and conclude at 5:00 p.m. I taught for five days and believe me it was probably the most intensive course ever taught through IU. After five days, I still had to figure out how to get home. At that time, no planes were flying and no one could leave the country. I waited for the time to leave. Throughout this time, I tried to get a message to my wife to no avail. Finally, I was able to board a plane to Teheran.

When I arrived in Teheran, I was informed that curfew was 9:00 p.m., and anyone on the streets after curfew would be shot. I left the airport and immediately went to the Hilton Hotel in the downtown area. No rooms were available so I made myself comfortable in the lounge. Curfew was lifted at 5:00 a.m., and flights were available to Athens. I paid a hotel employee to wake me at 4:30 a.m. and have a taxi ready for me at 5:00 a.m. Those plans worked out, and I made it to the airport at 6:30 a.m.check in at the desk for a boarding pass, I was told that I would have to pay a penalty fee. I questioned the fee, copied the agent's name on a piece of paper, stating that I would be back soon. He immediately gave me my boarding pass. At the same time, a family of four encountered the same problem with a requested penalty of $4,000.00. I made the same threat, and they received four boarding passes. I am certain many people paid huge fees to get out of the country.

Finally, my plane departed for Athens. Upon arrival, I immediately rushed for a telephone to call home, only to find out a telephone and telegram strike was in effect for Greece. What else could go wrong? Therefore, I did the next best thing—I caught a flight to New York City and then on to Indianapolis. Upon landing in New York, I called my wife and said "I'm home!"

In New York, I deposited an entire suitcase of letters into the mailbox. The letters were written to families from those who were still in Isfahan. I arrived at the Indianapolis Airport about 1:30 a.m. where I was picked up by our son, and arrived home by 3:00 a.m. Much of that day was spent making calls to persons who had loved ones in Isfahan. I should mention that this day was the Thursday in November that we call Thanksgiving. And indeed, it was the best Thanksgiving I have ever had! ⁂

Sounds of Time

By Henry H. Gray

I suppose that all of us can recall from early childhood certain favorite sounds, and I also suppose that the feelings such recollections generate are those associated with that childhood—feelings of fear or serenity, anxiety or happiness. My own childhood was particularly carefree (I know that now as I did not then) and so the chance memory of a sound of long ago brings with it a feeling of well being that is not easily achieved these hurried days.

Not one of my sounds of time, strangely, is associated with home. But only one in itself a sound related to travel. In 1927 I went with my family by train from our home in Indiana to the west coast. Because the trip took several days we engaged a Pullman compartment. I well recall watching the countryside glide by outside the window. I remember the smells of that trip too, and the crisp linens in the diner, and many other things. But it is the sound of a crossing bell that I never hear today without being transported back in time to my fifth year. Ding-ding-ding-DING-**DANG-DANG**-DONG-dong-dong-dong, louder, then softer it clamored as we passed with seemingly effortless quietness, and they always signified a grade crossing where we might see automobiles waiting impatiently for us to pass, or where at night we would see the brilliant flash of the red warning lights across our compartment window. The change in pitch of the sound as we passed fascinated me. I can now explain it scientifically and know it as the Doppler Effect whereby, among other things, astronomers can determine that all the stars in the universe are racing away from us at unimaginable speeds, but this more mature knowledge neither explains nor diminishes my feelings at hearing a crossing bell today.

My paternal grandparents lived in a fashionable part of Louisville. The avenue on which they lived was a quiet place, and especially so early summer mornings. The sun drummed at the windows of the room in which I slept when I visited there and wakened me at an hour that would have been unacceptable to the rest of the household, so I had to stay abed listening to the clock in the dining room downstairs as it softly chimed off the quarters, waiting for the first sign of life. Seldom did a morning breeze stir the leaves and even the Kentucky songbirds seemed slow to arise, so that my first indication that the silent world would awaken and my vigil would be over usually came with the milkman.

Louisville dairies delivered milk by horse-and-wagon long after most other cities that I was familiar with had changed to truck delivery, and none of those newfangled pneumatic-tired wagons, either. So each morning I listened for my unseen friend. The avenue was smoothly surfaced with asphalt but the side streets were brick, and the soft clip-clop of the horse's hooves increased to a clatter and then was suddenly augmented with a fortissimo jangling, rattling din as the wagon wheels, thinly tired with about an inch of hard rubber, rolled onto the bricks. Then, as abruptly as it began, the noises quieted as horse and wagon passed the corner of the house and I had to imagine that the horse would stop without signal, as I had seen others do, and would wait while the milkman took his wire basket of bottles to the back door. There he would be met by the cook, who would tell him how many quarts would be needed today (more than usual, because children were visiting) and would give him clean empties to be returned to his wagon. She might also favor him with a hot breakfast roll right out of the oven, but all this would be out of sight on the other side of the house and I could only imagine it, though I could smell the fresh rolls. The sounds of the daily milk wagon are gone from the street today, and gone also from most cities are the trucks that superseded them.

Another vehicle that is on the streets no more is the trolley car. My maternal grandparents lived in Terre Haute and the room that I usually slept in when I stayed there was high on the back side of the house and overlooked what seemed to be a vast sea of rooftops. Out in that sea, two streets away, was the trolley line, a single track with passing sidings every eight or ten blocks. My room had broad casement windows and even on the coldest nights they were thrown open wide. I crawled under heavy covers as the big steam radiator in the corner was turned off and the door closed; the fresh air would do me good, I was told. The bed was a wooden Victorian monster with thick octagonal posts, fully seven feet tall, highly ornamented with carved and pedimented designs and surmounted by a carved head from Greek or Roman mythology. There were two closets in the room and in the smaller one were shelves on which were kept toys and books especially for me. Surely there were other things in that room as well, but what I remember most about it is the sound of the trolley cars on cold winter nights.

The trolleys were called grasshopper cars, supposedly because they once were painted bright yellow-green (they were orange as I knew them), but they were small four-wheeled cars unlike the much larger eight-wheeled cars of the big cities, and as they went about their business they bobbed joyfully in a somewhat grasshopperly way. Larger cars also needed a conductor, but on these the motorman handled the car all by himself; when he came to the end of the line he got out, put up the trolley on what had been the front end of the car, got back in, closed the door, went down the aisle flipping the wicker backs so that the seats faced the other way, opened what was now to be the front door, got out, pulled down what was now the front trolley and hooked it down, and got back in. now he was ready to go back up the line whenever the schedule called for it. Even the switches on the passing sidings were arranged so as to need no attention from the motorman. Late at night, when only one car, the owl car as it was called, made the run down and back, the sidings weren't needed but the car had to go through the switches anyway. With few passengers the stops were infrequent and brief, and the owl cars seemed to cruise aimlessly up and down as if for fun, running only as far south as Hulman Street because there weren't enough passengers to justify going farther.

Sometimes, when I was downtown, I could hear the deep hooting blast of the air-horns carried by the big interurban cars, and I marveled at the variety of shrieks, howls, and ringing sounds made when the flanges of the big wheels bit at the rails on the sharp, street-corner turns where the tracks led into the terminal. These were muscular sounds, suitable for daytime only. The nights of which I speak were so quiet that in my room I could hear the cars from far away. First I could hear the slow tick-tack of the wheels on the rail joints, then the singing of the trolley wire, and finally the rattles of the windows and doors and the hum of the motors and gears. Now and then the car would shriek to a stop and the door would plop open to admit or discharge a lone passenger, and in the brief relative quiet I might hear the soft knocka-knocka-knocka of the air pump that powered the brakes. If the stop was long enough and the air reservoir became full I would hear in diminuendo the "psssssssss" of the relief valve as the pump shut off. Then the door would flap shut and with a sudden low growl the car would be on its way again into the night. On snowy nights that were exceptionally still, as the acrid smell of coal smoke drifted into my room, I might hear the trolley wire faintly singing long after all the other noises had been hushed. The automobile was on the scene but hadn't yet dominated it and few cars broke the silence of the cold winter nights.

These sounds of time are all but gone now. Can anything replace them in the hearts and memories of today's children?

**

Sun Yat-sen and I

By Leonard Gordon

As a graduate student in Taiwan studying Chinese, I saw Sun Yat-sen—not in person since he died three years before I was born—but his statue and pictures seemed to be everywhere. He could be found on stamps, currency, and in movies extolling his accomplishments. I also found his bronze image in cities on the China mainland and in North America, images epitomizing a man of intense conviction. In a Memorial Hall in north China, his basic ideology was carved in marble and painted in gold!

This leader of the 1911 revolution in China is revered in Chinese communities throughout the world. At first I found this adulation of Sun rather puzzling. His revolutionary effort to create a unified and lasting Republic in China was never completed in his lifetime. As the Republic of China's first President, he only controlled the southern half of China. In an effort to unite China after six months, Sun resigned and allowed a disreputable warlord to succeed him. Can you imagine George Washington setting a government in, let's say, Charleston, South Carolina, and resigning to give power to a dictatorial General in New York? Sun's action was no different than this fantasy.

Although Sun spent the remainder of his life organizing and writing in preparation for another round of revolutionary activity, he died without completing his objectives—to unite China and set up a modern, democratic Republic incorporating both Chinese and Western principles. In addition, Sun's

Nationalist Party and the Communist Party later engaged in a long and bitter civil war.

Despite Sun's failure to fulfill his goal and the failure of his Nationalist Party to govern China, he is a heroic figure in both China and on Taiwan. He is indeed an enigma wrapped in mystery. Perhaps it was the challenge to understand this curious man that led me to read and write about Sun Yat-sen.

What is the interest of Sun Yat-sen today? Next year, 2011, will be the 100th Anniversary of Sun Yat-sen's republican revolution. On the China mainland and on Taiwan plans are being made for extensive commemorations of Sun's life and contributions to China.

Most significant is that leaders in China believe that China and Taiwan can be reunited based on the ideology of Sun Yat-sen. The President of the People's Republic of China has often urged the government of the Republic of China on Taiwan to consider this path to a negotiated peace. If successful, it would lead to peace in the Taiwan Strait. If peaceful efforts fail, it could lead to war. The stakes are high, and I am working on this problem of reunification from the perspective of Sun's ideas.

Yes, I look forward to seeing Sun Yat-sen again! ✳

Shards

By Miriam Rosenzweig

Tradition has it that the Virgin Mary grew up in Sepphoris. If so, she could be expected to have been more worldly and sophisticated than her husband, Joseph, whose home was Nazareth, about an hour's walk from Sepphoris and a backwater in Biblical times. Sepphoris, in contrast, was an urban center where persons of many cultures rubbed elbows, exchanging goods, news and views. There are those who speculate that the young Jesus, working as a carpenter, could have been employed in Sepphoris, where he might have found the intellectual stimulation that led toward his vocation as a preacher.

Sepphoris is situated on a hill in Galilee midway between the Mediterranean and the Sea of Galilee. *Sepphoris* is the Greek name for the Hebrew Zippori, meaning like a bird. Its central location and good roads leading east, west and south, laid it open to trade, tourism and the mingling of peoples, as well as war, conquest, re-conquest, and turmoil. The city was conquered as early as the Assyrian occupation of Israel in the seventh century BCE. Subsequent Babylonian, Persian, Hellenistic, and Roman conquerors used it as a convenient administrative center.

Herod, appointed by Rome as King of the Judeans in 39 BCE, met with fierce revolt from the citizens of Sepphoris. He subdued them, then built one of his palaces there. Herod's son, Antipas, a more congenial personality, converted Sepphoris into a model Roman city during a massive building project that included a theater seating 15,000. Even

after the final dispersion of the Jews, a small Jewish population remained there for many centuries. The Sanhedrin, the highest Jewish judicial and governing body composed of eminent rabbis, moved to Sepphoris in the second century CE. This was a period of peace between Rome and her vassal city, making it possible for the rabbis to undertake the monumental task of compiling the Mishna, the body of law that became a part of the Talmud.

From the fifty century onward, the Christian population grew, accompanied by the construction of many churches. Following the town's conquest by Arabs during the expansion of the Muslim Empire in the seventh century, Sepphoris went into gradual decline. All that would have been readily visible to a tourist in the area at the beginning of the twentieth century was a citadel, built by the Crusaders in the twelfth century. They also built the Church of Saints Anne and Joachim. Though never mentioned in the New Testament, Anne and Joachim are names traditionally given to the parents of the Virgin Mary. The church was built on a site where their home was said to have stood, and where Mary would have grown up.

In 1930, the University of Michigan began archeological excavations at Sepphoris, and discovered the large Roman theater as well as another nearby buildings. With some lengthy interruptions, archeological work has continued there to present.

Among the most spectacular finds is a mosaic floor in the triclinium (reception and banquet are) of a luxurious villa, located near the theater. It contains a mosaic that covers the entire floor of the room and displays workmanship of extraordinary quality, with the use of small pieces of colored stone of many sizes and shades of color. One image depicts the fact of a woman of classical beauty, her features modeled in subtle flesh. So superb is her beauty that she has been called "The Mona Lisa of the Galilee." The floor is now protected by a roof and open to viewing by the public.

❊ ❊ ❊

When I visited Israel in 1994, a friend and I went to Zippori, while archeological work was in progress at a site that was the commercial center of the city during Roman and Byzantine times. Beginning in 1991, a team working on a large fifth century structure, uncovered exquisite mosaic floors in several rooms of the building. The floor of one room depicts fauna and flora associated with celebrations of the rising Nile River, and it has, therefore, acquired the name "Nile Festival Room." We watched work being done on this room from a nearby gravel path, a truly sublime experience. Suddenly, my friend bent down to pick up a small ceramic handle, apparently broken off an antique vessel. She handed it to me, saying, "Take it." I was shocked and protested that there was no way I would make off with Israel's antiquities, absolutely no way. She calmly put the handle into her own pocket book, as we continued to examine the beautiful plant, fish, bird and water scenes, laid out on the floor below us. I saw her bend down once more, but she knew better than to hand her find to me.

Mona Lisa of the Galilee, mosaic floor detail

On the way home, I received a lecture regarding ethical considerations, as well as rules pertaining to Israel's antiquities. Israel, she said, is virtually one huge archeological site, and in proportion to its size is carrying on a great deal of excavation work. As a result, the country has a surfeit of riches, and some artifacts are deliberately left behind because there are hundreds like them, already collected and in much better shape. That, she said, was the case with the shards on the gravel path. And, she added, had she not picked them up, they would have been ground to powder by the public trampling over them. I began to see her point.

When we reached her home, she showed me small artifacts she had collected over time, supposedly left behind at archeological sites. Some were shards, but others seemed remarkably whole. Perhaps she had stretched the rules a bit. In any case, her lecture had gradually changed by mind, and I was willing to accept her finds. She handed me the pieces and generously added a few more from her own collection. One was a smooth water-polished piece of ancient Roman glass. Like the glass, I had been honed down. I took my loot and returned to America.

Some years ago, I donated my shards to the Indiana University Art Museum, and it gives me pleasure to know that current and future students of art history and archeology can benefit from my bits and pieces of ancient poetry. ⁂

Nile Festival, mosaic floor detail

Faulkner Before "Faulkner"

By Walter Taylor

In 1948 I arrived fresh out of the army at the University of Mississippi. I was aware that the town of Oxford, home of the university, was also the home of a writer named William Faulkner. I knew little about Faulkner except that he was somebody I ought to know about. I had my own axe to grind, getting a long-delayed degree.

At that point Faulkner was just turning fifty. The period of his great works, which had gone largely unrecognized by the public, had ended with *Go Down Moses* in 1942. When I saw and heard of Faulkner in 1948 was from a time before he became famous. Before, that is to say, he became "Faulkner."

I knew that he was roundly hated in Mississippi. Much of that dislike came from the publication of *Sanctuary*, a novel about a Mississippi judge's daughter who is kidnapped by a voyeur, forced to live in a Memphis brothel and comes to like it. Jackson editor Fred Sullens called him "a purveyor of filth." The publication in 1948 of *Intruder in the Dust*, a novel about a Mississippi town so prejudiced that only a boy and an old lady can stop a lynching, did little to change that. The Ole Miss campus was segregated. A student editor who wrote that the South should be integrated was brutally beaten.

Knowledge of Faulkner came to me slowly. Among the things I did not know was that he was the grandson of the political boss of the county, and that his father was purser of

the university. William's photos from the era show a remarkably handsome young man with the broken nose he got as a five-foot, four-inch high school quarterback. He was crazy about his high school sweetheart Estelle, who left him for a wealthy young man. In World War I he dropped out of school and joined the Canadian Air Force. Several years later Estelle divorced her wealthy young man and married Faulkner.

Back in Oxford, Faulkner enrolled at Ole Miss, and later dropped out. He had a series of odd jobs, including an appointment as university postmaster. He was a disaster in this job, and he was more interested in reading books than filing mail, much of which he tossed into a waste can. He took to wearing spats and a monocle. Locals began referring to him as "Count No-Account." Moving on to the French Quarter in New Orleans, he posed as a combat veteran (he was not), walking with a limp and claiming that he had a silver plate in his head.

None of which was known to me in 1948. I would see him around town, driving his Jeep station wagon—a standing joke because he could barely see over the dashboard and worked the big steering wheel underhanded. He could be seen Sunday evenings joining his friends for dinner at a local restaurant, a rather quiet man with a graying mustache. And there were the tales of his drinking. It should be obvious, however, that no drunk could write the novels he had written.

Nor, for that matter, could anybody else.

During my senior year an incident occurred that could have been a career-changer for me. Looking for extra money, I answered an

Barbara Restle

ad for a student to help care for an elderly person. I knocked on the door of a modest, old-fashioned house. It opened and I could see no one. Then I looked down and there was a delicate, dark-haired lady who appeared to be in her seventies. She was one of the smallest women I had ever seen. In a sweet drawl, she identified herself as Mrs. Maude Faulkner.

Faulkner's mother! I know people who would have given an arm and a leg for that opportunity. I did not take the job. I wanted to graduate, and taking care of anybody, especially Faulkner's mother, was going to be a distraction. Or so I told myself.

Less than a year after my arrival at Ole Miss word spread that *Intruder in the Dust* was going to be made into a movie and filmed in Oxford. It was, to say the least, a strange situation. The town in the novel was fiercely prejudiced, and yet the town of Oxford and the ole Miss campus seemed somehow flattered. Students and locals lined up as extras to play the lynch mob. The University's all-conference linebacker was cast as a mob leader. It was a bizarre mixture of pride and prejudice. I was not sure about their feelings for Faulkner at that point, and I suspect they were not either.

In 1950 news came that the Nobel Prize committee had awarded Faulkner its prize for literature. It was a pivotal moment in Faulkner's public career. His acceptance speech would to be quoted around the world: "I believe that man will not merely endure, he will prevail." The speech caught the spirit of those Cold War times as none of his novels had. He toured the world as a spokesman for the State Department. His works, many of

which had been out of print, were back on the market.

He had become "Faulkner." ✲✲

ED deJEAN, a.k.a. MARK TWAIN

By Ed deJean

One of the most pleasant opportunities since Elinor and I moved to Meadowood was to share with the residents a side of me that they did not know. In July 2006, I asked Kathy Weigle, Activities Director, if she thought we could plan a birthday party for Samuel Clemens (a.k.a. Mark Twain) on or near his birthday, November 30. She thought we could. I asked her if Mark Twain could appear and speak at the party. She thought he could.

Should Twain's impersonator remain a secret until the performance? We decided that would be fun. I started to script his birthday address and learn his lines. On November 30, 2006, at 7:30 p.m., Mark Twain stumbled through the darkened Greenhouse, finally found the stage door to the Terrace Room, and introduced himself to Meadowood's "Respected Residents and Honored Guests."

How did I come to assume bits and pieces of Mark Twain as my alter ego? Over my lifetime, I have read the works of Mark Twain and literary criticisms of his writing. I came to be known in our community—Salem, Indiana—as a frequent quoter of Twain. In 1987, the Washington County Actors Community Theater (WCACT) selected "Twain by the Tale" as that spring's play. This was a production which featured selected writings by Twain—acted out. One problem presented itself; they could not find anyone who would agree to play the part of Twain.

One day, when I was out of the office and out of town, the play's director reached my wife Elinor at our home. He asked her if she thought they could persuade me to play the part of Twain? Please remember, I was not a real or self-imagined actor. "Oh sure," she said, "I don't see any problem."

I tried to escape, to no avail. They rented the show costumes. Mine was a baggy, white suit and the worst wig and mustache the trade could dig up. However, I did resemble Twain somewhat, when I got rigged out. Then came the surprise. When I worked my vocal cords just right, I could deliver a slow, crackly drawl. There are no recordings of Twain's voice. The Idiophone wax cylinders he once recorded have been lost. Who knows? I might sound like Mark Twain as played by Hal Holbrook. The play was a small town success.

One of my fellow cast members was Dick Russell, a preacher who has a great voice and true acting skills. Salem claims fame as the birthplace of John Hay, secretary to President Abraham Lincoln and Secretary of State under President McKinley. John Hay and Samuel Clemens were friends as young men in Buffalo, New York, where Clemens started married life while working as a reporter on a newspaper.

Dick Russell and I dug out from Twain's *Autobiography* some wonderful material telling about a visit by Clemens to the Hays in New York City. We converted it to a short skit, "Clemens and Hay," which we performed at Washington County's Old Settlers' Days in 1989. With a little praise, we were on a roll. Why not do a two-man play?

A deep lifetime friendship existed between Samuel Clemens and Rev. Joseph Twichell,

Pastor of the Asylum Hill Congregational Church in Hartford, Connecticut. (Refer to "A Tramp Abroad" by Twain) It was a perfect fit. Dick would play the part of Joe Twichell and I would play the part of Mark Twain in a two-man, two-act play titled "Sam and Joe." We started our research.

Early in 1993 Elinor and I visited Dick and Jane Russell near Dallas, Texas, where they had moved. Plans were laid for the basic plot of the play. Later that year I contacted the Mark Twain Project at the Bancroft Library at the University of California, Berkeley. The staff invited me to do research in their facility. Elinor and I flew to San Clemente, California, where we picked up Elinor's sister. We drove to Berkeley. There I spent a week in the Mark Twain's Project while they toured Northern California.

What a week that was: research material unlimited. I held in my hand leather notebooks which Mark Twain had held. I held the letter which John Hay had written to Samuel Clemens upon the death of Olivia Clemens. Letters from Joseph Twichell to Sam—on and on. We finished the play in 1994. We learned our lines independently. Dick Russell came to Salem in September and we rehearsed for a week. We did presentations in all the schools in Washington County and selected scenes from the play plus questions and answers on the life and works of Mark Twain. We registered the play with the Mark Twain Foundation in New York City and paid them a fee of $75.00 for permission to perform our copyrighted material. The WCACT group sponsored us for Friday and Saturday nights and Sunday afternoons. The admission fee was minimal, the audiences were adequate, Dick was great, I only "froze"

once, WCACT did well financially, and a terrific time was had by all.

Note: One disappointment—the play has not come closer to Broadway than the 786 miles from Salem to New York. However, you can read the play, and how it came to exist online at: http://www.twainweb.net/filelist/samjoe.html.

Immigration Tales

By Patricia Hassid

The Beginning of the Journey

I have always been interested in knowing how families who are not Native American came to be here, and why and how they came to leave their country of origin. Because we so often move on from our roots, we tend to lose track of family history.

My story begins with Josef Hassid, my husband's grandfather, who grew up in the city of Vilna, in the Russian Pale. Under the rule of the Czars, Jews were consigned to live in areas away from the interior, or in the far south, known as the Pale of Settlement. All Jewish male children between the ages of eight and twelve years were subject to compulsory military duty lasting from 5 to 35 years, in many cases, never seeing their families again.

Josef's father was an Orthodox Rabbi, and his native language was Yiddish. Imagine the terror Josef must have felt when, as a teenager, he was unwillingly seized, conscripted into the Czar's army, and sent south to the City of Odessa, near the Black Sea. There, he was taught to sew, and assigned to maintaining uniforms for the army.

Josef escaped from the army as soon as he was able and, hiding by day, and walking by night, made his way to Jerusalem. There he put what he had learned about maintaining uniforms to good use by setting up a tailor shop. He then sent word to his sweetheart, Hanna, who had been left behind in Vilna, along with her sister, Blume, actually walked across Europe to Jerusalem, where she and Josef were married and started their family.

Because of economic pressure, the family was forced to move to Cairo sometime after 1900. By then the family had grown to include three sons and a daughter. Once again, Josef set up a tailoring business, which eventually provided a living for him and his family.

Cairo

Josef's son, Leon, was the oldest of the three boys and the most dynamic. As a young man, he went to work for a newspaper in Cairo, while acquiring higher education. He then took a French law degree, and sent his two younger brothers to be educated. Once that responsibility was fulfilled, he started an import business as a manufacturer's agent for goods from Europe.

Eventually, Leon married Adele, a demure young Jewish girl with an infectious laugh, and quite beautiful. They were married in a Jewish synagogue in Cairo, and in 1931, their only son, Roger (who would be my husband), was born.

The years in Cairo were good to the Hassid family. Josef's tailoring business supported him and his family well enough, and his grown and growing sons all had successful jobs. Only his daughter Esther created a scandal in the family, because she fell madly in love with an engineer who was stationed in Zanzibar. She then went off to live with him in a tent (according to the family story). When Josef's beloved wife Hanna died, Josef came to live with Leon and family.

Things were not going as well, however, with the world around them. Increasing tensions arose out of the creation of the State of Israel, inflaming the Islamic population with a sense of dispossession, and widespread unrest that contributed to the torching of a synagogue in Cairo in 1948.

A good friend, who had immigrated to Cairo from Vienna, took Leon to the American Embassy to apply for a U.S. immigration visa. When Leon argued, "Why should I go? I made a good living here. Besides, I can't leave my father," his friend replied that it would not mean that he was required to go, only that he would be eligible for an immigration visa. He could send for his wife and son once he arrived in the United States. Leon went home and asked his son if he would like to go to college in the United States.

Coming to America

When Leon applied to immigrate to the U.S. in 1950, he didn't really plan on coming immediately—particularly since his father was terminally ill. However, the Egyptian Government forced his hand by nationalizing all of the businesses that were controlled by "Non-Arabs" (i.e. Europeans). This meant that he no longer had a means of earning a living. Regretfully, he arranged for his brothers to care for the ailing Josef, and he and Adele made plans to come to the U.S. as immigrants. By the time they were able to leave, it was the spring of 1956.

Tearfully, they said goodbye to the family and the way of life they were leaving behind, and departed for Genoa, where they had a four-day layover before they were to board the luxury liner, the *Andrea Doria*, bound for

New York. While awaiting their departure, they received word that Josef had died.

According to Jewish custom, the bereaved family must observe a period of seven days in which they do not leave home, but spend their time in mourning and receiving visitors. Because they were away from home, this period was spent in a hotel room in Genoa. Since the week of mourning overlapped with their departure date, they were forced to postpone their trip for a week and to relinquish their tickets for the ill-fated *Andrea Doria* which capsized and sank after colliding with another ship off the coast of New England on July 25, 1956.

The early years in the United States were not easy for the new immigrants. For Leon, there was the problem of finding a way to earn a living. Therefore, his early months were spent making contacts so that he could start over as a manufacturer's agent. Fortunately, English was one of the four languages in which he was fluent. Leon started out in Boston, where his son Roger (who had become my husband) was completing his medical training. Later Leon moved to New York City, and formed his own business selling classic German raincoats.

Five years after their arrival in America, Leon and Adele obtained American citizenship. Following the swearing-in ceremony, Adele turned to Leon, smiled sweetly, and remarked, "Now I am an American. Now I can tell you to shut up!" ⁂

A Serendipitous Phone Call

By Dan Osen

It was January, 1999. My wife had died six months before and I was in the midst of trying to figure out how to handle the rest of my life. My phone rang. It was the Associate Minister from my church with an odd request, "There is an old gentleman who comes to the church every day and sits outside my office, wanting to talk. I really don't have the time to do this and wonder if you would call him and see what it's all about".

The old gentleman and his wife had arrived in Bloomington in the middle 1990s from Afghanistan. He had secured apartment housing here and was employed by the Monroe County school system helping physically-challenged students on and off school buses. His health failed and he was not able to continue work. When I contacted him, his only income was picking up pop cans and selling them.

How did this couple end up in such dire straits? The family had been living the good life in Afghanistan. He was a news media employee, schooled in journalism, and she was an elementary school teacher. Their departure from the country was not planned. He had uncovered a scam which he reported, only to find out the authorities were a party to it. He and his family were literally burned out of their home compound and fled by foot, over the mountains to Pakistan. Some of the members were separated from each other during their flight. The old gentleman

and his wife finally made it to the United States by some means not shared with me.

I brought the situation to the attention of a group I belonged to at my church. We agreed to subsidize their meager income temporarily to allow for them to pay their rent and have food on the table.

By this time he and his wife had been in the United States for five years and were eligible to apply for citizenship, so I set out to learn how this could be accomplished. After many phone calls I found out where to get the application forms. The forms were extremely complicated for me to fill out. Imagine what filling them out would be for a person with limited English! After many months the applications were approved and the swearing-in ceremony was held in Indianapolis. Citizenship allowed them to receive Social Security but only a meager amount so we continued to help them out financially.

Shortly thereafter, we were informed by them that a daughter-in-law and her four children, who had escaped to Pakistan, could be brought to the United States if a sponsor were found. I agreed to sign the papers of sponsorship and they arrived in Bloomington as refugees in August 2001. We found them housing and she, a former high school teacher, subsequently found employment at Indiana University. The husband, a ranking member of the judicial system, remained in Afghanistan as a political prisoner. He escaped from the prison in late 2001 and made his way to England.

Our group did our best to help the mother and her four boys feel welcome. I even became a "soccer-dad"; well, at least a "soccer-grandpa"! They picked up English quickly but found many of our idioms puzzling. One of the boys came to me with a question; what is this business of "butterflies in the stomach-it sounds awful!"

The husband finally made it to the United States and he, too found employment at Indiana University. They are now all United States citizens after months and months of paperwork going back and forth from us to the various government agencies. The immigration office for this part of the United States is in, of all places, Lincoln, Nebraska. One would not think of Lincoln as a port of entry!

In time, they qualified for Habitat Housing and are fastidious property-owners.

The two older sons will graduate from college this spring. The third son is graduating from high school this spring and the fourth son will be a high school junior this fall. The four boys are excellent students. The family is a very worthwhile addition to our great country.

Notwithstanding the success they have obtained, it is impossible for most of us to realize the high price they paid along with way for their freedom!

Now, tell me, was that not a serendipitous call I received in 1999?

An observation: After executing the mountains of paperwork required for citizenship I can see how an alien, without a sponsor or an advocate, finally gives up and goes underground to become an illegal alien.
**

Miller-Showers Park: Gateway to Bloomington

By Julie King

"The Earth Day Massacre of 2002" . . . "An Environmental Disaster" . . . these are two examples of the invective aimed at a public space just south of the bypass, between College and Walnut. It may have been the most controversial public works project in Bloomington's history. How this space was transformed into "Indiana's largest rain garden" is a remarkable story of persistence by leading citizens and city planners.

On a sunny March morning in 2011, a dozen or so Meadowood residents set out to explore Millers-Showers Park. Wellness Coordinator Alyssa Hinnefeld had advertised this hike as an easy .6-mile trek on paved walkways, perfect for the reluctant (like this writer.) I had driven by the park many times without taking in its complex interplay between water, plants and technology.

As we stood on the large pier next to the parking lot, the ponds looked very tranquil with two mallards feeding at the edge of one and another mallard snoozing on a concrete abutment. We could see how the four ponds descended like stair-steps toward the north where a u-turn driveway provides access to businesses on the east side of Walnut. Water lilies were spreading across the waters, and bulbs were pushing up along the walkways.

Later in the summer prairie plants like black-eyed susans and coneflowers would emerge. Signs told us how each pond provides a different habitat for sediment and pollution control.

Taking in this peaceful place for the first time and recalling the heated debate about its construction, I set out to learn about the evolution of Miller-Showers Park. The name "Miller-Showers" refers to the site's provenance. In 1929 the city's first park board paid $1 for land originally known as the Jacob and Loretta Miller Homestead. There were two deeds: one between the city and the Showers Brothers Furniture Company, the other with the Miller family. The purchase of the 15-acre site included a requirement that the land be used for a park.

Ted Deppe was the founder of the Parks & Recreation Foundation and its president for 30 years. (The Foundation has raised many dollars over the years for park projects and for scholarships for youngsters to attend special programs.) Ted recalls the many meetings called to develop the Miller homestead site. Everyone agreed that the location should be an attractive entry into the city and not necessarily a place for traditional recreational activities. Ted calls the Miller-Showers Park "a beauty spot". A plaque dedicated to his accomplishments was placed in the park at the time he retired from the Foundation.

Doris Brineman's late husband, Don, was a vice-president of the Foundation. Doris remembers his working on a report about major problems at Cascades Park north of town. Cascades, established in 1924, was Bloomington's first official park. Don was concerned about Cascades Creek's badly-eroded channel, the frequent flooding of park roads, and oil, dirt and trash polluting the creek. All this was the result of uncontrolled drainage of storm water moving northward from downtown over a 20-block area. It turned out that the solution to Cascades' problems lay in the Miller-Showers property.

But over seven decades, little was undertaken on that site, other than some playground equipment, a bench or two, a puzzling statue, and plantings that pleased few. About half of the storm water from downtown Bloomington was crossing Miller-Showers via a narrow channel leading to Cascades. Erosion and soggy ground made the location a park planner's nightmare. Zetta Ann Weaver's family moved to 19th and Walnut in 1947. Zetta Ann lived there a year before she married and moved west. All she remembers are the weeds. She and her family thought the park a very ugly place for visitors passing by as they entered Bloomington.

Today there is a sign at the entrance proclaiming "A Park With A Purpose". Water occupies almost 2 acres—1.2 million gallons. A collection chamber under the pier holds large debris. Weirs with waterfalls separate the ponds. Aquatic plants and underground sediment traps begin the cleaning process. Water jets push algae downstream. The flood plain at the north end with its prairie plantings slows and cleans the water moving through an underground culvert towards Cascades Park.

Citizens were outraged when 66 trees were removed from the property to prepare for construction of the current park. The "Earth Day massacre of 2002" is long-forgotten now that 300 native Indian trees and 28,000 native plants have been added. A 2006 Indiana University research project showed that pollutants at different locations throughout the Park had been reduced by 64 to 75 percent. The Park now meets or exceeds EPA standards for storm water treatment and is much more cost-effective than a treatment plant would be.

Ask park visitors what they think about "the park with a purpose." Their reviews might be "Visionary" . . . "Impressive" . . . .

Not to be missed." As for those two limestone statues at either end of the park, that's a story for another day. ⁂

My Little Red Purse

By June Miller

I carried my little red purse when my Mother and I boarded a bus that would take us from Indianapolis to Los Angeles. The time was the beginning of the Great Depression 1929 and I was seven years old. Mother and I were following my Daddy and spending as little money as possible, and that meant traveling by bus and not by train. I had no idea what it was going to be like traveling on a bus for a long journey.

At the bus station we boarded our big bus, and found that the large windows had no screens, which meant they could not be opened. It was a close situation with no storage for luggage inside the bus. The only place for my little red purse was in my lap. Before we left home, Grandma had given me twenty-five pennies for an emergency. The driver put all our bags in the bottom of the bus. Just before we left, the driver passed out some candy to us, then sat down in his seat, honked the horn and at last Mother and I began our adventure. In a short time I also found out there were no bathroom facilities on the bus and learned I had to wait for the next stop in our journey. I also found out there was no food available until we got to the next stop. If I remember correctly, the only food available for those six days of traveling was hotdogs.

Now remember, the bus traveled all night. And the seats did not have the capability of placing us in a reclining position. Mother and I learned to sleep while sitting upright. The main topic of conversation was who was going to see the mountains first. I do remember that before we arrived in Denver we caught a glimpse of Pikes Peak. By that time we had been traveling three days and three nights and eating only hotdogs. At Denver, the driver told us we would be sleeping in a hotel. He probably thought we would all need a bath, and so did we. Up to Denver we had only traveled on gravel roads and this was also true all the way to Los Angeles. This was Route 66 in 1929!

For the next three days, until reaching Los Angeles, we only stopped for food and bathroom stops and refueling of the bus. We passed through Albuquerque, Santa Fe, Raton Pass, Oatman Pass and into Needles, California on the border with Arizona. Just as the sun was setting over the mountains, we arrived at the bus station in Los Angeles to be greeted by my father's smiling face. And, of course, I had not spent any of my twenty-five pennies in my little red purse. ✳

Christmas Tree Adventure

By Chuck Rockwood

When Christmas approaches, I am reminded, as we all may be, of Christmases past. In the early 60s, the cost of getting a tree for the family struck me as ridiculous and I decided that someone was making big bucks in the process. I figured you planted them, cut them and sold them at a huge profit. Accordingly, I ventured into the business.

I bought seventy-plus acres on Birdie Galyan Road for eight dollars an acre—a sizeable investment for an Army major stationed at Fort Knox. With the help of the local soil conservation agent, I proceeded to plant ten thousand scotch pine seedlings each year for the next seven years. All was well and good, and I visualized profits sprouting with each tree until the moment reality set in and I realized one must mow to eliminate weed competition, and, worst of all, each and every tree must be pruned to ensure proper size and shape. This whole operation took care of all my spare time and energy!

The first season, I had some trees ready for market, I cut three hundred of the best ones and shipped them to Fort Knox by hiring out-of-season limestone haulers with flatbed trucks. They were well received and sold like hotcakes. Encouraged by this success I decided to branch out and expand my market to Florida. So the following year, I sent two truckloads to selected Publix grocery stores in Florida, and once again they sold instantly. I was on a roll. Publix was so happy, they gave me an order for three thousand trees to be delivered next year to selected stores around the state.

I won't bore the reader with the agonizing details, but will only report on the disastrous results! Truckload after truckload *en route* to Florida encountered ice and snow with tons of salt—salt that got thrown up on the trees and immediately turned them brown. Needless to say, you do not fight Publix super markets, and I think for the whole agonizing experience I netted some six or seven hundred dollars! The only thing that saved me was Lady Bird Johnson and her highway beautification program—but that can be a subject of a later tale.

Thor—Up Close and Personal

By Robert F. Blakely

When neighborhoods are new, they are full of children and have many vacant lots. At the time that we moved with our two children into the Bloomington subdivision of Park Ridge, that was the way it was. Almost every home had children, and vacant lots were handy baseball diamonds.

It was a cloudy spring Saturday morning when young ball players began to congregate in a vacant lot on Smith Road near the railroad underpass. Soon there were enough players to form two sides, and I was appointed the umpire, not for my judgment but because of my lack of baseball skill.

It was a good-sized lot for baseball, and the game flowed along nicely. Everyone was engaged in the game and did not notice that the clouds which had been small and thin had, by now, become more numerous and dense. There were no warning raindrops, however, and play continued without anyone yelling "Kill the umpire!"

Suddenly I felt an unusual sensation: every hair on my body stood straight up in the air. Looking around at the players, I could see that all of them were experiencing the same feeling. Sensing that it was atmospheric electricity, I yelled, as loud as I could, "Get down." Everybody quickly dropped to the ground. We had no sooner flattened out on the ground than the earth gave a great thump as though it had been hit by a huge sledge hammer. Immediately our hairs dropped to

their normal state. Slowly, everyone began to stand up and look at each other in surprise. Someone yelled "Let's go home." Everyone took off, some slowly in wonder, some fast in fear.

Back in the safety of our home, I reasoned that an electrical charge had built up between the overhead clouds and the earth and had jumped the gap between the sky and earth without enough energy to have caused a lightning flash and the resulting thunder. We had simply felt the thump of the transfer of energy as we lay flat on the ground. What might have been a tragedy ended as a memorable event.

Barbara Restle

Bougie—Une Chienne Tres Extraordinaire

By Naomi Osborne

The day I was born, my father presented me with my first puppy (concealed in his coat pocket.) From that time on, a love affair has existed between me and dogs. At some period or another, our family had a variety of them—different breeds, sizes, colors, sexes and temperaments—all very much beloved. None was ever bought: either they were gifts or rescued from animal shelters or were abandoned ones who, like hobos, turned up at our door, somehow sensing they would not be shooed away.

Of all of them however, the one who was most outstanding and an indelible part of my life was a beautiful black poodle named Bougie (meaning a candle or live battery.) She was what the French call a Caniche, being slightly smaller than a Standard Poodle.

She came into my life in the former Belgian Congo (now Zaire). It was the time of revolution when Congolese were killing Belgians, raping nuns and robbing anyone available. My staff was worried about my safety since I worked late at night and traveled alone. They said I needed at least a dog to protect me.

I had visions of a gaunt, mange-ridden bad-tempered Congolese dog and said, "No, thanks!" But several days later they presented me with Bougie. She had belonged to a Belgian couple who had fled the country. They had turned the dog over to the young Swiss living with them with the plea to give her to someone who would love her as much as they did.

For weeks the dog was coldly aloof, responding immediately to all my commands, but looking at me as if to say, "Do you call that French?"

All the while she was grieving for her master and would run up to any car with a white male driver and then turn away with ears and tail drooping when she saw a stranger. She would stand over her food for hours looking at me for the command to eat; only when her hunger was so intense would she finally taste her food. It was obvious that her Belgian master had taught her a key word for eating to protect her from Congolese who first poisoned the dogs when they wanted to rob a house. (My French friends and I never found the word.)

One night I returned home very late. I had not eaten but was so weary I had no appetite. During this period, food for us had to be flown in, grocery stores shelves having long been emptied. Since I was rather skeletal by this time, I thought I'd better eat something. Then I remembered that the Procurement men had brought me back some French Roquefort cheese from across the river in French Congo. I decided to eat some cheese and drink a Congolese beer, good and plentiful.

I sat eating the cheese and drinking the beer when I heard a shuffle by my side. To my surprise, there was Bougie, the first time she had approached me. "Bougie, you don't want this—its cheese," I said, extending a piece I was about to eat. Whereupon she daintily took it from my fingers. For a half hour, we ate the cheese together and I drank my beer.

From that time on, she was my dog and no one got in my apartment, house or hotel room unless I said, "its okay, Bougie" (that is, unless he or she wanted an ankle enclosed in strong jaws).

We went all over the world together on our various U.N. assignments; on tramp steamers or ships, on her first trip by airplane out of the Congo which nearly caused her to suffocate (she was put in the non-pressurized hold with the luggage). She became famous wherever we were, not only because of her beauty but also because of her high intelligence and devotion to me. She was the darling of models in fashion shows, on television, on a magazine cover and in newspaper articles.

Many interesting stories were told about her. One of the ones I like best happened in Trinidad. My maid Wilma had a boyfriend Fred who was a taxi driver and whom Bougie adored because he bought her ice cream cones and took her in the taxi whenever possible. Word from several sources began to float back to Wilma that Fred was seeing another woman—that they had been seen joyriding here and there—a fact that Fred denied. One day when Wilma and I went grocery shopping we caught up with Fred's taxi. Wilma gasped, "There she is!" As we passed the taxi, I glanced in and there was Bougie snuggled up to Fred as close as possible with her head leaning on his shoulder. With her French topknot from the rear of the taxi she looked exactly like a woman with an Afro hairdo out with her man!

A woman once said to me, "I don't consider poodles dogs; I think of them as "Little People." I'm sure Bougie never considered herself a dog. She was so extraordinarily special that perhaps, after all, she was just a small person in disguise.

**

An Introduction to Global Warming

By Terry Loucks, Ph.D.

As a fiscal conservative, it bothers me to leave a federal debt for my sons and grandchildren. I had no idea that I was also leaving an environmental debt to them. As a scientist, let me explain.

Before the industrial revolution, there were only 280 parts per million of carbon dioxide in the atmosphere. Now there are 380 ppm, or an increase of 35%, thanks primarily to coal and oil emissions, which are dramatically increasing today. Coal is used globally in many power plants while oil emissions come from transportation.

Isn't carbon dioxide harmless? Don't we exhale it every breath? Yes, indeed, but it is also a greenhouse gas, which means that, along with methane from our cattle and rice fields, it is warming the planet faster than any time in our geologic history.

How do we know that? From direct measurements and from both land and ice cores that go back hundreds of thousands of years. The temperature in the past hundreds years, even though it is still rather tolerable, has increased at record rates.

The previous record for the Earth's rate of increase in temperature was right after the last ice age, and today it is increasing thirty times faster even than that. Thirty times faster than the previous world record!

In the distant past, 200 million years ago, there was too much carbon dioxide from volcanoes, leading to a major extinction. Even so, the temperature did not rise anywhere near its present rate.

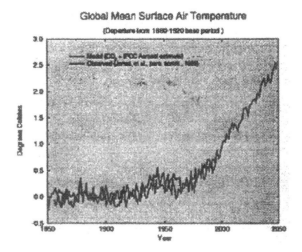

We can see this in a graph of temperature over the past 150 years. This information is amazingly available for hundreds of thousands of years, but I am only showing you fairly recent data. Computer models, similar to the ones used to forecast hurricane paths, have been used to predict the next fifty years and the results, also shown on the chart, are terrifying.

If we do not stop dumping carbon dioxide into the atmosphere our grandchildren may well be doomed. The insidious thing about this gas is that it stays in the atmosphere for about a hundred years, and there is already way too much in there for the good of mankind. Ideally, we should be taking some out if we only knew how.

The challenge humans face is that our normal "wait till the last minute" politics, fight or flight reactions, will just not work. If we stopped today, which would indeed be a miracle, our children and grandchildren would still have to endure the hundred-year lag time from the carbon already there.

Meanwhile the oceans, which end up with about half of our carbon dioxide emissions, are becoming too acidic for life, and at the same time the fresh water from melting polar caps is threatening the Gulf Stream.

We are playing with fire, called carbon dioxide, and it is an inheritance we had no idea we were leaving to our grandchildren.

*
**

LOVE IN OLIVE DRAB

By Alfred Diamant

I heard the news about the attack on Pearl Harbor at a meeting of the Jewish fraternal organization B'nai Brith, which had taken me under its wing from the time I first arrived in Taunton, Mass., from Europe in 1940. My American sponsor Abe Diamond managed a textile mill there. I was put to work in the mill less than a week after landing in New York City. In the two years I worked for Diamond Textile Mills, my wages generally hovered around the federal minimum wage of $15 per week—or 37.5 cents per hour. If that would suggest that I felt like a slave laborer that would be far from the truth. My weekly bill for room and board was $12, leaving me all of $3 for my other needs. Yet in those two years from my arrival until Pearl Harbor, I was content with my life and clearly happy to have reached the United States. If I was indeed an exploited worker, my working class consciousness was poorly developed, despite many years of membership in the Austrian Social Democratic Party.

The day after the attack on Pearl Harbor, a Monday, I went to my draft board and asked to be called up for duty immediately. I had been classified 1A, a fit specimen of American manhood. I was inducted on January 15 and entered into a very strange world indeed. I was instructed how to make my bed and spent several days taking tests. The tests seemed to indicate that I had unusual mechanical abilities and I was, therefore, ordered to report to Fort Knox, Ky., the headquarters of the armored force of the U.S. Army. I could neither drive a car nor tell one end of a motor from another, something missed by the first tests.

However, the ordinary human beings who staffed the training sessions soon found me out! All this did not disqualify me from further military service, but it meant that I should not be trusted with anything as valuable as a 2 1/2 ton truck. So I was ordered to an open field where there were a number of Harley-Davidson motorcycles and several unfortunate sergeants who were ordered to teach me to ride one. Eventually they succeeded, and I was ordered to ride on an open highway where traffic seemed to consist entirely of big trucks that threatened to eat alive any unfortunate motorcyclist who might cross their paths.

I have little recollection of the rest of my basic training period of eight weeks. What I do remember is that everybody else in the training company received orders to report to one or the other of the armored divisions—everybody, that is, except me. The commanding officer of the training company decided if nobody else wanted me, he could make good use of me when the next group of recruits reported for duty. I was promoted to the rank of corporal, and I still remember sitting on my bunk and sewing the two stripes of a corporal onto the sleeve of my dress uniform.

Just as I was in full swing bellowing at recruits (most of them seemed to have two left feet), the company received orders for transferring me to Fort Benjamin Harrison in Indianapolis. The order referred to Private Alfred Diamant; my captain assured me that my rank as corporal would eventually be restored. I wept as I sat on my bunk, taking the rank insignia from my sleeves. My captain guaranteed me that the order for the transfer was issued before the ordered for my new rank was received at higher headquarters, but I was sure that some sort of snafu would eventually deprive me of my new rank. But the captain was right, and I was wrong.

With my restored rank, I was freed from the miserable duty of riding in a garbage truck guarding people who might be trying to escape. I was assigned to the company's supply room and began to learn the intricacies of Army regulations. After a short time, my superior, the supply sergeant, was transferred, and I was promoted to staff sergeant. Thus, I had not only my original rank restored, but added two more stripes.

In my frequent trips to the post supply room, I came to know the clerks who would process my applications for supplies. That is where my life took a very decisive turn. During one of my frequent visits to submit a requisition for supplies to the quartermaster office, there was a young woman behind the desk whom I had not encountered before. When my turn came, I submitted my application and stood quietly while she scrutinized it. After a while, she stopped reading the application and looked up at me. As she relates in her memoirs, she found Sergeant Diamant "a most ridiculous figure . . . . He wore a uniform that was too small for him, a soft hat that was also too small, and he spoke English with a decidedly German accent." Fortunately, this initial impression did not doom me in her eyes.

Her name was Ann Redmon, a native Hoosier, one of the many civilians working on the post. She had been reading many books that dealt with international relations and wanted to hear what I had to say on the subject. This happened every time I went to the quartermaster office. All this led in seemingly casual steps to lunches on the post and eventually to evening dates that ended up not in a bar, but in Indianapolis's finest sweet shop. What I remember, even after 60 years, is a red velvet dress that shaped her body beautifully.

During the fall of 1942, I noticed an announcement for a recital by the pianist Rudolf Serkin. Without asking Ann, I bought two tickets and presented them to her upon my next visit to her office. Many years later, she confessed to me that she had already purchased a season ticket that included the Serkin concert, but she accepted my invitation without hesitation anyway. Both of us have long since agreed that the Serkin recital was a decisive element in our subsequent relationship. Such dates continued throughout the fall. They came to an end in mid-December 1942, when I was ordered to Fort Knox for officer training: I was scheduled to become a 90-day wonder, an officer and a gentleman.

The days at Fort Knox were long and demanding, but I continued to be so excited about the prospect of being an officer that I lived through those days without much thought of anything else.

As February arrived it brought with it that holiday seemingly so important to women, Valentine's Day. It puzzled me, because I didn't really understand what it was all about, but I knew a gift would be expected. I couldn't go into Louisville to look for a present for Ann, so I was limited to the selection at the PX. In the end, I selected some Swiss lace handkerchiefs, mailed them to her, and left her totally puzzled as to what the gift might mean.

When it was certain I would graduate, I wrote to Ann to ask her to come to the graduation ceremonies. At first she pleaded that her work would not permit even a day off, but eventually she relented and attended the ceremonies. On the following Sunday, she needed to take a train to return to Indianapolis so that she would be at work on Monday morning. I decided to accompany her to Indianapolis and get a hotel room. I would then decided what I wanted to do with my 10 days of leave. That train ride changed both of our lives forever.

According to Ann (my own recollection being rather fuzzy on this point), on the train I suddenly turned to her and said, "I want to get married." She replied archly, "Do you have anyone in mind?" I told her that she was the chosen one. There followed a long discussion about the wisdom of marrying during wartime with all the uncertainties, including my possible death in combat and all the other lesser fears produced by war. I finally told her that she ought to think it over and take all the time she needed to make a decision—but to be sure to let me know before we arrived in Indianapolis. When we arrived, she consented to be my wife, and thus began our 60 years of love and companionship.

**

Born in Vienna in 1917, Alfred Diamant came to America in 1940 to escape Nazi persecution. On December 8, 1941, he joined the U.S. Army and later participated in the D-Day invasion of Normandy. He attended Indiana University on the GI Bill and has graduate degrees from Yale University. Professor Diamant taught political science for 25 years at Indiana University.

Tilling

By Edgar deJean

Today, as I was tilling our garden with
Our bright red, Troy-Built 6.5 hp Super
bronco Tiller,
I heard the angry twang of tine against rock,
and
Immediately a sharp ping that meant
"A stone in the starboard dirt."

I released the safety handle, the machine
stopped
And I stooped to search out the intruder of
my loam.
As I wiped the dirt from the flat stone, slightly
smaller
Than my hand, a wave of desecration swept
over me.
I held the tool of a Native American polished
by
Years of use and the oil and sweat of his/her
hand.
It was perfect but for two ugly gouges along
one side.
In two milliseconds tine one and tine who
had spoiled
What years of shaping arrow points or
cracking nuts, and
Centuries of soil entombment, had failed to
harm.

For 50 years I've gardened this pot on our
two-acre lot,
Cleared from a primeval forest almost 200
years ago,
Later carved from a cow pasture to be our
homestead.
As rains fell on the tilled earth, chips of
flint,

Not indigenous to the area, would surface
and find
Their way to my garden collection that
contains
Chips and some imperfect arrow points. It
also contains
A mate to his stone-age tool, perfectly
polished and
Free from the ugly scars gouged by a 6.5 hp
modern tiller.
Hence my guilt upon desecrating what was
precious,
Yes, even life-giving, to a former steward of
our garden.

Time to time I shared the secret of our
garden,
And when a young man, courting the girl
next door,
Went away to State University to study
archeology,
He reported our garden to the Archeological
Powers
Where it was registered as Indiana Site 12 Ws
43.
This meant that it was the forty-third site
recorded
In Washington County, Indiana.

Often as I struggle with the insignificant
problems
Of my garden, which is a hobby backed up
by the
Security of the supermarket two auto miles
away,
I think of the hardships of my Patch of
Earth,
Native American, Spirit-Mate. I think how
fragile
Was his/her existence in the same spot where
we hold
Freedom from fear and want and where our
power tiller

y

36 | Barbara Restle

Can scar the beauty of her/his hand-polished,
vital tool.

As I contemplate the hereafter, would that it
be one in which
We might meet and I could say, "I'm sorry I
scarred your hand tool.
We regret immeasurably that our people
scarred
your people."
**

A Brief Cross-cultural Encounter

By Violet Chiappetta

There I was sitting alone on a massive carved stone, looking out over a field of shaped stones extending as far as the eye could see. Some were arranged in shapes such as a door, others looked like a wall and many were strewn haphazardly on the ground. It was a silent place except for a man in the distance talking earnestly to two people who seemed to be listening intently. The man was likely a guide explaining to his two guests the glories of the Inca past.

Feeling a bit faint (the altitude?) I was happy to sit quietly as the sun's warmth penetrated the cold air around me. This place was Sacsahuamán, famous Incan ruins located high in the Peruvian Andes. It had been a village and probably a sacred place, where the Incan Empire celebrated victories, prayed to please its gods, and administered its vast domains in Latin America. In the end the Incan Empire was destroyed by the Spanish conquistadors.

As I sat quietly contemplating the scene, I noticed among the stones something moving toward me. Finally two young native girls, surely descendants of the Incas, stood before me, one carrying a bundle. Since they spoke Quechua, and I English, with a smattering of Spanish between us, communication was sure to be difficult.

As we spent time examining each other we heard the drone of an airplane above us. I recognized it as a plane from Lima belonging to Faucett Airlines which regularly flew from Lima into and across the Andes and to the Amazon jungle on Peru's eastern border. The older girl, pointing to the plane and then to me seemed to be asking if I had come in such an object. I nodded yes. When she used a word in Spanish that I thought meant "frightened," I said "No, flying in an airplane does not scare me." That was only partly true. Whenever I flew into a valley in the high Andes or to a village in the Amazon region, breathing through a slim oxygen tube provided on the Faucett plane, I admired the magnificent views below me, but I was constantly aware that only a thin strip of metal separated me from the forbidding scenes below.

As I watched the plane head toward Lima I felt something tickling my leg. I looked down to see the younger girl stroking my leg. She pulled back, frightened, so I smiled broadly at her, a universal sign that no offense was taken. My guess was that she had never felt a pair of silk hose and wanted to see what they were like.

Finally the girls indicated that they would show me what they had in the bundle. When they carefully unwrapped it, I was looking at a baby peacefully sleeping in its haven. I recalled learning in Lima (a rumor?) that Indian women sometimes sold their babies in native markets to foreigners. I murmured a few words of admiration but said nothing more. In the uncomfortable silence that followed the girls finally wrapped up the bundle and disappeared as quietly as they came.

Barbara Restle

They returned to their world and I to mine. But even now, decades later, my thoughts stray to those two girls and our attempt to reach out to each other. ✿

Something about Angels

By Robin Black-Schaffer

Some people have Angels; I know at least two who do. One, I think, is an Angel, although she may not know it. Maybe she never will, but I do.

How can it feel to have an Angel of one's own? Would it be like having a sibling? As an only child, I've often wondered about that; but it seems most people have siblings, and rather taken them for granted. I don't think one could take one's Angel for granted.

Could it be like one's imaginary playmate? I had one of those for awhile. Whatever became of him? Anyway, in retrospect, he was really an echo of me; I always had to take the initiative.

My imaginary, yearned-for identical twin, maybe? I did so want to have someone entirely close, entirely mine, entirely Me. But I'm no angel, so my identical twin surely wouldn't qualify.

An Angel must be so different: standing outside of oneself, and yet more inward than one's deepest thoughts. Does it guide? Protect? Comfort? Warn? Make secret miracles?

Do some Angel-ed people want to get away from their Angels sometimes—like a bad conscience?

Perhaps all my friends have Angels: perhaps I'm the only Angel-less person that I know.

Think of it: an Angel who knows one's inmost thoughts, one's secret heart!

How do I *get* an Angel?

BUT—WAIT A MINUTE . . .

Think about it: this Angel knows my inmost thoughts, my secret heart!?!

Do I really *want* an Angel?

400 Million Years . . . And Counting

By Barbara Restle

On a recent Friday, 8:00 a.m., my dog Sam and I walk along the banks of Griffy Creek, two miles north of Meadowood on Dunn Street. We have made this walk every morning for two years. On this morning, as usual, Sam has his large nose skimming the dew-covered grass, sniffing out the previous night's wildlife escapades. Last week he sniffed at an opossum lying upside down in a tangle of weeds, pretending to be dead. I touched the warm body and Sam showed little interest in it. This land is part of 6,000 acre watershed of Griffy Reservoir. On this morning after several weeks of drought there is no water flowing over the concrete spillway of the dam of Lake Griffy.

I am, as usual so early in the day, before a cup of tea or coffee, barely conscious of my environment. My brain is in limbo. My brain is in neutral. I particularly do not want to think about what is going to happen to me in five days. I definitely do not want to admit that I am frightened about what will happen to me in five days.

As I have done every morning for two years, my eyes seek out the small fish in the creek. I see a few bass, some small and vulnerable. And then I see a very large creature floating, not swimming, just below the surface of the water. It is about four feet long. The shape is fish-like and that is all I can describe. I see flimsy fins fluttering. The color is a strong shade of blue. I see two tiny glistening eyes, like pearls, on either side of what looks like a foot-long paddle-shaped head—or is it a mouth? The eyes are positioned so that I believe each eye might be able to see 180 degrees. This means it might be able to see what is behind it.

We have been in a drought with the creek so shallows that this creature is without a doubt, trapped. In front of this fish-like creature is a very thick and tall growth of exotic water plants that biologists have tried to poison this summer and behind this creature, there is nothing but rocks sticking out of the water.

I have never seen a fish like this. I assume it is a fish only because it is in the water. I watch as it works hard to keep its head positioned into the slow-flowing water. In less than a minute I see it is floating backwards toward the rocks. With a jerking motion it moves its body to face upstream to keep from being impaled on the jagged rocks. The creature is struggling. For some reason I find that I feel distressed watching this perpetual attempt for this large fish to maintain this exact position in the shallow creek. The banks of Griffy Creek are only 15 feet apart.

On Saturday morning, at 8:00 a.m., Sam and I begin our daily walk again. We approach Griffy Creek and I look again for the small local fish. I am sorry to see the large blue fish is in its exact same place in the creek. Again I watch its struggle to maintain its position in the shallow, rock-strewn water. I feel a higher level of distress. I now know this fish is trapped. I had hoped the weatherman would indicate rain. But the drought continues and the water level is dropping.

This morning, I know what I am looking at. It is called a "Paddlefish, *Paleodon Spathula*." My books indicate that it has not changed in any way, whatsoever, in 400 million years. This fish predates all the dinosaurs. On my computer I have accessed all the information I can possibly integrate. In my college years, I took Biology 101 and Zoology 101 and knew I would never manage to become a scientist. My computer reports that in the Yangtze River, the Paddlefish reaches 21 feet and is killed for its eggs, caviar which apparently is a much sought-after delicacy.

In our country, the Paddlefish has been found in the Ohio River and has been caught by biologists at 16 feet in length. For me to have seen something so endangered, and even threatened, right here in our Meadowood backyard, astounds me and worries me and I am beginning to feel a responsibility to it. Only a few days ago, I found evidence of irresponsible behavior of local fisherman when I found a large pile of small bass dumped in the grass. I feel a sadness and helplessness.

Sunday morning, the Paddlefish is in the same place.

On Monday morning, my fourth sighting of the Paddlefish, I stand beside it and know I have to do something. An unwelcome noise of a motorcycle jarred me into turning towards the parking lot and a large young man in white overalls walks toward me. I hope it is not a local fisherman.

"Hi Barbara, a great morning to walk Sam." It is Chris, our painter at Meadowood. I point to my fish. "What is that? Biggest fish I've ever seen." I tell him all I can about what I have learned and tell him I am worried that it is trapped and that there is no let-up in the drought. He says, "Well I think we should call the Department of Natural Resources or some agency." Chris continued to look at it and we are both quiet for some minutes. "Well, I gotta get to work, lots of painting to get done," and he leaves.

I call a federal biologist at the local U.S. Fish and Wildlife Office, and in a little more than one hour, two U.S. Federal Wildlife biologists and two Bloomington Parks and Recreation personnel arrive at Griffy Creek. After a few words of exclamations they don their wet suits and all four men, using long nets enclose the fish, lift it into a large plastic tub. The men explain that they plan to drive the fish to deeper water to the north. I ask, "Where?" They say they will release it into Bean Blossom Creek adjacent to a 700 acre land trust refuge; the one next to wetlands with the name RESTLE at the viewing platform.

The next day I am in the hospital for the scheduled major surgery. And still no rain has fallen. I think about Paddlefish swimming towards the White River, to the Wabash River and back to the Ohio River. For some reason I cannot explain, I am no longer fearful for what lies ahead for me.

How I Discovered Mt. Fuji One Morning

By Luise David

After thirty years of working in the textile business in New York City, I retired; that was the year Edith Frank and I made a memorable trip to Japan where I came face to face with Mt. Fujiyama, the holy mountain. This was truly a high point of all the wonderful trips we took together.

Edith and I met, seemingly, by chance. I had become a widow, and in 1962 my daughter Susan and I moved from Brooklyn to 382 Central Park West in Manhattan to begin a new life. Susan and I lived in apartment 6J and, although Edith's apartment, 5B, was across from us, I had no opportunity to meet her because our work schedules were so different. Edith taught chemistry at Bronx High School of Science; her classes started at 8:00 a.m. and she was finished with work by three in the afternoon. I left later in the morning and came home after 6:00 p.m.

In our apartment building, neighbors on their way to work or school often became familiar with one another while waiting for the elevator to stop on our floor. One chatted about the weather or gossiped a bit about other tenants. That is how I learned the woman in 5B seemed to have the same interests as I. My neighbors kept urging me to get to know her, but our paths never crossed.

Then one spring, when I was home from the hospital recovering from an operation, I happened to return from a walk in Central Park around 3:30 p.m. and stopped to admire our building's new outdoor plantings. A lady I did not know also stopped. When I went into the building to pick up my mail, the lady followed and opened her mailbox, as well. She turned to me and said, "You must be the lady in 6J who everybody tells me I should meet." It was Edith Frank.

Our friendship started with plants. Edith and I got into a lively discussion about the new outdoor plantings, and this led to indoor plants, which we both enjoyed cultivating. She invited me into her apartment, and when I admired her thriving Swiss Ivy, Edith immediately gave me a cutting. I reciprocated by giving her a cutting from one of my plants. From plants we branched out into other mutual interests. Soon we were sharing dinners, going out together to concerts, plays and museums.

When summer rolled around, we began to travel together. Over the years, we planned our trips with great care, even visiting Israel four times by combining various tours. One year, with the assistance of a midtown Manhattan travel agency, we worked out an ambitious Japanese tour, which would end with a visit to Mt. Fuji.

The trip began memorably. Edith had been to Japan a few times before; however, the route we took was new to both of us. On Japan Airlines we flew non-stop to Tokyo, via the northern route, which meant flying over the North Pole and skipping a day—a concept that sounded quite unreal to me.

Once in Japan, we traveled from place to place on a famous bullet train. One can write a letter on this train while it is in motion—it is such a perfectly calm and quiet way to travel.

Passengers do not feel the tremendous speed with which they are being transported.

The travel agent had planned our tour to include Hiroshima, Hong Kong and several other cities. Near the end of our tour we were in Tokyo, looking forward to spending the last few days of our journey in a hotel at the base of Mt. Fuji. It was afternoon before we found a taxi and driver who motioned a 'Yes' when we gave him the name and address of the hotel. After our bags were placed in the trunk, Edith and I felt we could sit back and relax. Little did we know what we were in for.

Afternoon turned into night. It was pitch dark as we drove through several small villages in what seemed a hilly terrain. I felt we were going up and down on serpentine roads. There were valleys and high rising mountains that seemed taller than the ones we had just left. A bright full moon appeared. Now we saw the moon on one side of the taxi, and then on the other side. We were both too exhausted to talk. But suddenly Edith started to shout at the driver that he was taking us the wrong way. I tried frantically to calm her down and explain why she was seeing the moon changing sides, but she was adamant and kept shouting. The driver paid no attention—just ignored her and kept on driving because he did not understand English.

Finally, we came to a clearing and saw our hotel in the moonlight. By this time Edith had quieted down. I paid the driver from both our wallets; this ride cost $160. After I registered, a bus boy picked up our luggage and led us to our room, where the blinds were drawn closed. The beds were a welcome sight, and I tipped the young fellow. As soon as he left, we slipped out of our clothes and sank gratefully into our beds.

The next sound we heard was a knock on the door; a waiter entered and opened the door to the balcony, where he set up our breakfast. When I stepped out on the balcony, I saw a breathtaking view: Mt. Fujiyama was straight before me in brilliant sunshine with not a cloud in sight, its snowcap sparkling doubly bright.

We had been told in Tokyo not to feel bad if we could not see the entire sacred mountain because most of it is usually hidden behind clouds. Visitors travel to this park from all over the world, but rarely get to see the beauty of Mt. Fuji as we were seeing it. Edith, too, was speechless. We took in the exquisite view for a day or two until we had to journey back to Narita Airport and home. ✳

The Lone One

By Henry H. Gray

The figure at the door of my cabin seemed scarcely more substantial than the timid knock that had announced it. An ill-fitting blue shirt and ragged denim trousers, well faded from an overdose of Idaho sun, all but concealed the slight feminine aspects of her figure. Wrinkled lace boots, rolling weakly outward at the heels, and a yellowed and drooping cowboy hat with string ties completed her costume. She rolled the ties onto her finger and off again as she spoke.

"Pop took my dog out and shot him. Could you drive me to the Falls? I can pay you a little for your gas." I looked at her tear-stained face for a few seconds. "You sure you want to do this?"

"Oh, yes, yes! I've been thinking about this all day. I'm all packed. I'd hitch-hike, but there ain't many cars this time of night." Her brown eyes were bloodshot and her black hair was even wilder than usual. "Please?" she implored.

Well, I thought, she's no kid, she's old enough to know what she's doing. I turned to the figure sprawled on the upper bunk. "Come on, Fred, let's go to the Falls," and moments later, the three of us in the front seat and her small weathered cardboard suitcase in back, we rolled through the gates of the cabin camp and out into the empty night. The single night-light at the gas station next door soon faded into blackness behind us.

"We had an argument. Pop said I paid more attention to my dog than I did to him. Then he took my dog out and shot 'im. That was just after lunch. I haven't seen 'im since."

She and her collie had been the only occupants at the camp when Fred and I had moved in, some weeks back. Her cabin was right next door, and so we sat on the porch of an evening we had noted that she wasn't the usual tourist. She was small and not bad looking, in a rough, rawboned sort of way. Apparently her worldly goods consisted of her dog, the worn denim clothes that she constantly wore, and perhaps one dress. Once during the summer we had seen her in that dress.

"I don't hate Pop. He's the nicest old guy I ever knew. He was really nice to me. Paid my rent, bought my groceries, everything. We went riding and hunting and fishing all the time. But I loved my little dog, and Pop shot 'im!" She blinked hard to spread the tears around a bit.

Fred and I had observed that Pop spent a lot of time with her. Pop owned a ranch up the road, but he ate all his meals on the porch of her cabin, and through the evening they talked or played cards or just sat and watched the world go by. They kept pretty much to themselves and didn't talk much with us or with the other occupants of the camp.

"I'm mad at Pop but I don't hate 'im. His wife is dead and he hasn't got nobody, nobody but me, that is, and I guess I ain't much. I've just got to get away and think. I really loved that little dog; he's the only thing I ever really loved."

The collie had certainly been her constant companion. He was as small for a collie as she was for a woman, and he could curl up on her lap as she sat on the porch of her cabin. These scenes flickered through my memory as I sat between Fred and the girl, while Fred wheeled the car through the night at a steady 60 miles per hour.

"Here," she said, suddenly pressing a silver dollar into my hand. "Maybe this will help pay for your gas. I'm sorry I can't give you something more for your trouble."

"That's O.K." The dollar was moist and hot, and seemed to burn in the palm of my hand. "What are you going to do when you get to the Falls?"

"I don't know. I keep coming back to where I started. Nowhere. Nothing." She paused. Then just a little more brightly, "Once I worked at the hospital. They liked me there. I hope they can take me back. I sure need money, I won't last the week."

"Won't Pop find you?"

"He won't know where to look. Don't tell him, please? Maybe he'll find me some day, and maybe that's all right, but right now I've got to be alone. I've got to think. You married?" The abruptness of the question startled me and I gave a surprised half chuckle as answer.

"Ha! I thought so. Marriage is hell, isn't it? I was married once, guess maybe I still am. We both loved fishing and hunting and riding. But it didn't work out. We just fought all the time. And we hadn't any money and we lost our little ranch. I don't even know where he is and I hope I never see 'im again anyway.

But I guess it's my fault too. I don't much like to cook and keep house, I like to be outside. But I ain't gonna change!"

She threw that last sentence a bit defiantly at me. Well, no use telling her, I thought. I missed my home, my family, and I didn't much like being gone for the summer, but teachers need summer jobs. But why tell her this? Let her get what consolation she might from her idea that all marriages were hell, maybe many of them are. Mine wasn't. She'd had only her dog to love, and now he was gone. Fred's face remained impassive, eyes on the road. Half way there, 40 miles or so, and we'd met only one car. Was that the way with this western vastness, a breeder of lonely people, perhaps?

She talked on and on, between sobs. A carefree life as an only child on motherless ranch, little formal schooling, riding herd with her father, no sense of growing up. It would always be this way, she'd thought. I sat beside her, only half-listening, nodding, now and then and answering briefly the short questions that really needed to answer. Thirty-something she might be, alone and completely adrift. The unhappy early marriage, the log home on the little ranch, she was glad they'd had no children. Pop had wanted to marry her, but she'd said no, once was too much. She hadn't talked this much in all her life, maybe, and thanks for listening. But promise not to tell Pop anything, please.

Her cascade of memories continued until the twinkling lights of the city appeared in the distance, then tapered off into whispered, halting phrases that stopped as she began to feel the impact of what she had done. The lights grew closer and now winked past the

Barbara Restle

car's windows. "Where do you want to go?" I asked.

"Oh, just let me off at the theater," she replied in a very thin, lost-little-girl voice.

"Sure you don't want to go back?"

"No! I'm sure," her reply shot back with almost a touch of bravado. "Right here will be just fine." The box office was closed but the marquee was still bright. She stepped out onto the sidewalk and I climbed out and took the suitcase from the back seat and put it in front of her. It was surprisingly light. "Now go on!" she said. "I don't want you to see where I'm going."

"Here," I said, pressing the silver dollar into her hand. It was as hot and moist as before. "You'll need this. And good luck, Mary." I had learned her name at the general store but had never before had cause to use it.

"Thanks," she choked, as tears again streamed down her face. There'd been so many I couldn't imagine there could be any left. "Thanks a lot. Now go on. And don't tell Pop!"

"Sure thing. Good bye!" I got back into the car and we drove off. As we rounded the corner I looked back. She was still standing there, small in the flickering lights on an otherwise darkened street, hadn't even picked up her suitcase. And then she was gone, as our headlights again tried to split the infinity of the Idaho night.

***

A Letter to my Daughters

By June Miller

Today, as I sit here at my desk and look out the window at our cardinal family, watching their caper—their humorous first flights, their feeding, with the mama hovering close—I couldn't help but think of you as my own little birds who have now spread your wings and flown the nest . . . and I'm rather like the mother cardinal. I tried to make your lives more comfortable, happy, and warm, with lots of tender loving care. Like the mother cardinal, I popped the first bit of food into your eager mouths, helped you take the first steps that would carry you through a lifetime . . . your first flight into a busy world. Now you've really flown away, to begin what you said would be a new life—exciting, and far removed from the rest of the family.

I guess this letter will be the means of telling you something I've wanted to tell you for a long time . . . just how much you have given me. For you see, we've grown up together. Life with you has not only enlightened you, but it has taught me and given me so much.

I learned patience—for just keeping your busy and inquisitive hands and feet still in order to accomplish dressing you required this. Patience, in realizing that one day you'd learn to say "Please" and "Thank you."

I learned compassion and sympathy—for whenever you came to me with a bump on your head or a skinned knee, I learned to give you a sympathetic pat and squeeze . . . I learned how to feel sorry for you.

I learned to appreciate the beauty that surrounds us, for how could I resist your "oh's and ah's" over a new violet that had popped up overnight, the bluebirds when they nested in our redbud trees, the wonderful look of pure joy when our kittens were born.

I learned to laugh—at you and with you. I learned pride—in you and for myself, because of you. I learned to pray—for when you were ill, when you wanted something special, when you needed guidance, I prayed for you. And I'm certain God answered these prayers.

And yes, I learned that God really is: For when I looked into your eyes, heard your laughter, saw your beauty as it grew into bloom, how could I doubt that you were anything less than God's gift to me to love, to nourish, to teach, until the time should come that you no longer needed me to teach you, for you were already established on the right road of life. Your own experiences, and your own children will continue your education—as you did mine.

Yes, you've gone . . . not from my heart, for that couldn't happen, ever. Somehow, knowing this, I feel secure and extremely happy . . . glad to tell you what I've learned by being . . .

—*Your Mother*

✲✲

June Miller is a star, sparkling and talented. She had her own TV shows in Indianapolis and Toledo. She has been a realtor and now is an inspirational speaker.

The Tomato: A Reverie

By Miriam Rosenzweig

I have a flower bed in which no flowers grow. I've tried annuals and perennials of many kinds, but soon after they are planted, they turn a sickly color and die. Suspecting my soil might be deficient, I tested it and found that it is too alkaline. Over time, I began applying peat and other acidifiers, but nothing helped. One year, I gave up, deciding to leave the bed fallow. But as I was leaving the greenhouse, loaded with plants for my more cooperative flower areas, I saw some vibrant young tomato plants, and, on an impulse, purchased one.

I planted it in the offending flower bed, fully expecting it to keel over and die, as all the other plants had done. But within a week it looked as though this plant intended to defy my expectations. After two weeks it had grown into a healthy, deep-green plant, and as time passed, it grew upward and outward, soon occupying the entire bed. It began sprouting blossoms, some turning into tiny fruit.

I watered and fertilized my young charge and checked on it upon waking every morning. Without my willing it, the tomato became this summer's major focus (not to say obsession). When a painter came to paint a fence near the tomato bed, I impressed upon him the importance of not spraying paint or trampling my plant. I think I drove him crazy, but he did his job without doing harm. So did another workman, whom I drove equally crazy. The tomatoes grew large and round,

and, as luck had it, the first fruit turned fully ripe on the day my two daughters came for a visit. It was placed on the menu for that evening's dinner.

The Hebrew prayer book contains many blessings for all occasions and every vicissitude of life. One of the blessings is to be recited upon seeing or doing something for the first time, including the consumption of the year's first harvest. Although my family is not given to religious observance, I suggested that we recite the "first fruit" blessing, just because it seemed appropriate. The girls went along with it, and together we gave a full-throated rendition of the blessing. Roughly translated, it says:

> Praised be thou Lord,
> King of the Universe,
> Who has given us life
> Sustained us and allowed us
> To reach this day.

Then we shared the fruit, which was juicy and rich with flavor.

That's the story—hardly worth telling. While others spent the summer traversing the world, deepening their insight and broadening their horizon—I grew a tomato. But I don't want to drop the matter without pondering the meaning of my experience. What unrecognized need did the tomato fill? What was it that resonated so strongly with my inner self?

All of us are living with the consequences of life accelerated by technology. Computers govern the speed at which offices strive to operate. In order to comply, humans must do several tasks at the same time, a phenomenon for which we invented the term "multi-tasking." But human evolution has not kept pace, and we are not, in fact, capable of multi-tasking—witness the many glitches that accompany our interactions with organizations of every kind from gas companies to banks. Just a few days ago, the Lehrer News Hour carried a segment devoted to the vanishing verb. Governed by the "sound bite," another recently coined term, newscasters can't afford to speak in whole sentences, and often drop the verbs, the analyst observed.

The tomato, in contrast, operates at its own pace. Its visible progress is measured in weeks, not nanoseconds. I can't push a key to accelerate or delay its growth. If I wish to live in harmony with my tomato, I must fall in with its leisurely tempos. And when I complied, the process turned out to be calming and serene. Others achieve serenity through meditation, yoga or jogging—I grow a tomato.

While tending to my plant this summer, I thought of my paternal grandmother for the first time in many decades. She died before I was of school age, and I have only one recollection of her. My mother and I took a train from Munich to Berlin, where she lived in an apartment. I remember it was enveloped in bleak darkness, accentuated by her black, ankle-length dress. This atmosphere of gloom was offset by several red tomatoes, which grew in boxes on her balcony. My sturdy tomato, thriving where nothing else grows, unexpectedly connected me to my forbearers.

We are often told that we are fouling our earthly nest at ever-accelerating speed. Perhaps the tomato will be around to nourish humanity when other, less hardy, plants have vanished.

⁎⁎

My Hill Town in Italy

By Nancy Martin

I have spent magical time each year for 34 years in my house in a hill town in Italy, Civita Di Bagnoregio, about an hour's drive north of Rome. It is in the Lazio region (which for many years was part of the Vatican) and about five miles from Umbria and ten miles from Tuscany. In 1973, my daughter (Carol Watts) was a graduate student in Architecture at the University of Washington and was in a Rome program for the spring semester. Her professor had recently bought some property and was restoring it in Civita. She had an option to buy some adjoining property. She wanted to use her money for her own renovations. However she wanted to control this property so the professor encouraged Carol to buy the adjoining house and write her master's thesis on its restoration. I flew over that summer by myself with the money. I loved Civita and also decided Carol was too committed to back down or her academic future would suffer.

Vittoria and Luigi Rocchi had lived all their lives in Civita and had inherited this particular property with deeds going back to the 1400s. The site had been continuously inhabited since at least 600 B.C. An upper cantina (cellar) has been identified as Etruscan and a lower cantina as Roman. There is also a Roman cistern. The three-foot thick stone walls of the house were built in the Middle Ages between the 11th and 13th centuries.

The Purchase Contract specified that the Rocchis could live in the lower part of the house for their lifetimes. Vittoria is still going strong at 95. Carol restored the upstairs with one entry room below. She duplicated a door found in a cantina where it had been for 20 years when the door had been filled in with masonry. It is forbidden to change any exterior visible from the street but you can replace a door that once existed. She added plumbing and electricity and took off part of the roof for a roof terrace. Carol stayed in Civita for five months, mostly by herself, directing the renovation. All materials were brought up the hill on mules.

The garden on a steep cliff was used at that time for raising chickens and vegetables. An earthquake in 1695 caused part of the town to fall off the cliff. Our garden is on the edge of that cliff where once there were houses, and their exposed basements are in our garden. One had been made into an olive mill.

Over the years this has been transformed into a beautiful flower garden with a grape pergola, marble tables, a loggia (part of the mill) for rain or shade and a fireplace for grilling. The lowest level of the garden is a small vineyard.

Carol and her husband both teach architecture at Kansas State University and spend a lot of time in Civita. They recently converted a hayshed on the top garden level into a modern garden house with a window wall, a fireplace, a small kitchen and a bathroom with a magnificent 50-mile view. This garden house is where I have stayed the last two summer visits.

In 1973 Civita was called the city that was dying (Il Paese che Muore) because the only access was impassable for automobiles. The government was encouraging the inhabitants to leave and was threatening to cut off all water and other utilities. Most of the people in the town did not want to leave. In a few years however, the town turned around and outsiders started buying houses and restoring them.

It became a hot jet-set spot for a few years with several millionaires making lavish restorations and bringing staff. Now with the exception of a few old families, it is a second home for most (mostly Italians, especially Romans). My niece and nephew from Virginia enjoyed visiting me so much they both bought houses as did one of their friends. I enjoy family reunions when we are there at the same time. We are the only Americans except for Carol's professor husband, also an architect, who has retired there. Carol's professor, Astra Zarina, died a few years ago.

About 20 years ago the Rocchi sons who had moved away became interested in Civita and open a Bruschetteria—they take turns each week and their entire families help. Before my husband died we arranged to give our property to Carol—an adventure in itself. There are property taxes on changes of ownership based on an appraisal but very low annual fees. Twelve years ago we realized how important it was to have an Italian presence looking after the property and sold back to the Rocchi sons part of the downstairs of the house (that Vittoria could live in for life) but reserved a bedroom. Carol plans extensive remodeling when it is available.

I have been in Civita every year except for three years since 1973. All of my children and grandchildren and many friends have enjoyed it. My Italian was never great but necessary in the early years. Now many speak English. We are good friends with all the local residents and many of the other outsiders. It has changed because we get so many tourists, perhaps a thousand a day on busy weekends now—a lot of Italian tour groups. Fortunately they are there only between 11:00 a.m. and 6:00 p.m., so it is quiet in the morning and evening. A lot of schoolchildren from Italy come. It is like a "Williamsburg" because it is medieval and there are no automobiles in the narrow Roman-era streets. There are about 14 residents in the winter and about 100 in the summer. The climb up the hill on foot takes from 10 to 20 minutes. The climb is the equivalent of a 10-story building, about one-quarter mile. Special arrangements can be made for residents to be taken up in a special vehicle. Every year and every season is different. The Festas are fantastic and there are occasional art and music programs in the Piazza. Movie makers love the setting, and of course the wine harvest is great fun.

It's a magical town. It is completely free of any pollution. The view from our terrace and garden is protected by the same historical preservation laws that keep us from changing the exterior of the house. No change can be made in the valley or town and new development is forbidden. The Italians know their main industry is tourism. Each year I'm completely immersed when I am in Civita into an entirely different culture—language, food, wine, and meal times. ✳

The Golden Book

By Dee Rockwood

The Golden Book, or book of deeds, is an extremely large bound book handsomely displayed in the Memorial Room of the Indiana University Memorial Union. The book records the names of the men and women who attended I.U. and then served in the wars of the republic. It records members of the University who served in the War of 1812, The Black Hawk War, the Mexican War, the Philippine Insurrection, the Mexican Border Expedition, and World Wars I and II. *The Golden Book* is hand-lettered, in part, by my hand.

I taught myself the art of calligraphy while in high school, and was soon able to put my skills to use. In the mid 1950's I hand-lettered in Old English lettering certificates for many I.U. departments, one of them being the Alumni Office. The Alumni Office presented certificates to their alumni club officers statewide, Emeritus Club, and many others. My dining room table became my cottage industry workshop in the evenings after my young children had gone to bed.

The task was a little complicated for I left the certificates on the dining room table overnight to completely dry in order to avoid smudging when I erased the lines in the morning, before the children were up.

After a year or two, Claude Rich, the Alumni Secretary, asked me if I'd do a lettering job in *The Golden Book*. I was thrilled and agreed to letter 10,000 names of men and women who had attended I.U. before entering military service during WW II. I had six months to complete this job and was to be paid $1000.00!!! Can you imagine $1000.00 in the 1950's!!!!

Soon a huge bound book arrived at my home along with ten or more shoe boxes filled with index cards which held the 10,000 names of the military persons. I was to write these names in script.

If the person had been killed, then I was to print their name in Old English lettering and write a sentence or two about them, branch of service, degree held, etc. A gold star was to be placed above their name.

The *bound* book, (and I'm stressing bound for the pages didn't come out) was large, heavy and difficult to handle. And the pages were completely blank. It was quite a difficult and time-consuming job to line the pages in pencil, making sure the lines were level and precisely spaced. Then I did the lettering. As with the certificates, I erased the lines in the morning after I was positive the ink was dry. Then I put the book on the top closet shelf for safe keeping until the evening. If a mistake happened, a drop of ink or a misspelled name, I'd carefully scrape the error with a knife and rewrite the name.

I worked nearly every night for an hour or two until my hand cramped or my eyes began to see double. I had calculated that if I lettered two pages per night, I'd finish the job in plenty of time. I did finish the book on time, and bought new carpeting for my living room!!!

Now some 50 years later, I'm so pleased to have been involved in such a valuable historical project for I.U.

Until a few years ago *The Golden Book* lay open in the Union Building and a page was turned daily. Now it is housed in a locked glass case and the pages cannot be touched. If you are interested in seeing a particular name you must ask at the Information Center next to the Memorial Room. ⁂

When in Rome

By Irv Danielson

In 1968, I was the Manager of European Operations for Thor Power Tool Company, then an 80 percent owned subsidiary of Stewart-Warner Corporation. Thor had three subsidiaries in Europe—in England, Italy and Germany. Germany was a sales company with about 80 percent of its manufacturing operations in England, where I lived.

We had lost our local manager in Torino, Italy and I was making my first trip there to fill in while I found a replacement. I was greeted by a union demand that I approve a 7.5 percent increase in wages or they would strike at 9:00 a.m. I knew that our wages were competitive and we paid a performance bonus on which they were earning about 20 percent. They were having me on!

Our Italian company made air-powered tools, primarily for FIAT and a new car manufacturing plant in Russia. The bulk of the work was "metal working" and the custom was for a worker on strike to stay at his machine. Ours was a new factory, all on one level.

I sent word to the union that "I was on strike, too" and went to the center of the factory, folded my arms and changed my direction about every 15 minutes so I could face all the workers.

At 11:45 a.m., the union sent word that "if I would go back to work, they would go back to work." The strike was over.

Many of the workers kept a bottle of homemade wine in their lockers and at lunch one of them brought a glass of his wine to my table and we "saluted" each other.

As the Bard of Avon wrote, "All's well that ends well."

⁂

Memories of China

By Eleanor Byrnes

President Obama's recent Asian odyssey brought back vivid memories of my trip to China with my husband in May 1981. Bob was invited to speak in China from Harbin in the north all the way down the coast to Shanghai in the south. Arriving in Peking we were met by our two contacts who would travel with us during this month. Driving in from the airport it was dark, and cars did not use lights at night, just dimmers. We toured the city for a few days and we viewed all the important sites as well as seeing ladies with bound feet, stores fully stocked, and bicycles galore. Cars were mainly Russian, Japanese, as well as Chinese. Drivers turned off their motors most of the time and coasted.

When our tour ended in Shanghai we returned to Peking where arrangements had been made for us to continue on to the People's Palace where the body of Madame Soong (Madame Chang Kai Shek's sister) was lying in state. A state limousine with red curtains was waiting for us, but my husband thought it inappropriate for him to go. They requested that I go, and I did. The limousine deposited me at the entrance to the Great Hall of the People where soldiers in long lines on both sides of the building were approaching, two by two, up the front steps of the entrance. They inserted me and my contact into the line and we continued up the steps. At the top we were directed to a table with large squares of parchment for special guests to sign. A black armband was placed on my left arm, and we proceeded into the Great Hall of the People. There was a large backdrop with a huge picture of Madame Soong in the center, and overhead in large Chinese characters—In Memory of Madame Soong. On either side of the hall, in double rows, were huge wreaths set on standards. Her body was on a catafalque and enclosed in glass with the flag of China draped over her body. Beneath and around her were wreaths.

All of a sudden the lights went on and my picture was taken. We walked behind a group standing nearby and proceeded out the way we entered, stopping by the table to leave the armband. The limousines returned me to my hotel.

This is a notable memory of my visit to China. ⁂

A Musical Family

By Ledford Carter

Richard Wagner (1813-1883)

Hans von Bulow, a pupil of Franz Liszt, became one of Europe's best pianists and conductors. He married Liszt's daughter, Cosima. Richard Wagner appointed Siegfried von Bulow conductor of his operas in Munich. Wagner then took Cosima as his mistress. When Wagner's first child, a daughter by Cosima, was born, von Bulow accepted her as his own. When von Bulow's marital problems became well known in Germany, Cosima still refused to return to him.

The public outcry over Wagner's extravagance; morals and his dominance of the king, forced him to leave Germany. He and Cosima, with a full allowance, took up resident at the palatial estate of Tribschen on Lake Lucerne in Switzerland. There, Eva, a second daughter, was born. When Cosima bore Wagner a third child, Siegfried, von Bulow had enough. He sued for and was granted a divorce. Wagner and Cosima were subsequently married at a church in nearby Lucerne. To celebrate the birth of his son and Cosima's recovery from childbirth, Wagner composed and premiered *The Siegfried Idyll* at Tribschen. Tribschen is now known as the Wagner Museum, and I visited there in 1981. Wagner returned to Germany to select Bayreuth, Bavaria, as his residence and home of the Wagner Festival Theatre. This site for the preservation of performance of his works has been managed in modern times by one of his descendents.

Thither and Yon

By Jean Herrmann

We are under way! The deck of our freighter, "The Hogue Merchant," is already dipping and rolling. Streamers of foam follow our progress as a sturdy little tugboat forges on ahead.

Boston Harbor fades behind us, and now our ties to the homeland are severed. Who would have believed that I, Jean Herrmann, a native of Bloomington, Indiana, would ever find myself on the deck of a freighter, accompanied by a husband and two little boys, and on the way to Pakistan! Not I! No, though I have longed to travel and experience the unknown forever—well, at least since I read *The Royal Road to Romance* by Haliburton. My husband, Joyce, is no stranger to travel. The son of Methodist missionaries, he has traveled the world over. Once and a half around it! There he is, racing over the desk with two little fellows in hot pursuit. He looks carefree and boyish. I know that he is drinking in great draughts of sea air as he finds his sea legs. He is in his element. And why not, since he is a Navy man? But now a gong is ringing, and we must go below to ready up for dinner.

To our surprise, we find that the children are not to dine with us. Now is the time to explain that there are only nine passengers aboard, and four of them are children. Two sets of parents and a medical missionary on his way to Cairo complete the roster . . . and then there is the captain's new wife. She counts more as staff, since she has decided that she must set the protocol and enforce it rigorously. She is a charming Australian: pretty and likeable, but determined to assert her authority. For beginners, we shall dress for dinner every evening of this momentous voyage. Barbara and Bill Peacock are the parents of a son, four years old, and a daughter, Susan, two and a half. We have two sons, George, age five, and Bill (known as Winkie), also two and a half. It is probably because we are well matched as to age and our destinations of Karachi and Lahore that we were assigned to travel together when our other travel arrangements broke down. The ship to which we were originally assigned has met with some sort of delay which has not yet been explained. Neither was it mentioned to us that our ship is returning to Norway for repairs by way of around the world. Also unmentioned is the news that the previous captain's ten year old son was lost overboard on the last trip. We shall be attended by a small group of officers and a crew of Guyanese stewards who speak no English.

This night will always be remembered as the Halloween that wasn't. This favorite family day would have been spent at home trying on costumes and decorating trick-or-treat bags. Not today. We must rush our children into quick baths and make a beeline to the galley, where they will eat in high chairs that have been lashed to the table with leather straps. The food is plentiful and attractive but a little much for confused children. A few mouthfuls and they are sated. Wind and sea air have taken their toll, and we must put them to bed without offering a single Halloween treat.

Barbara and I check the portholes and hastily climb into our finery. We arrive at the dining room to find all the others assembled. Her highness has been seated

Barbara Restle

and is waiting. Our husbands look at us a bit askance for the delay, but still we demand to know what the arrangements are for guarding the children. It seems that no one has given it any thought. The captain agrees to have a steward sit between the two cabin doors. Now we sit down to a sumptuous dinner.

Dinner is followed by a bridge game for four avid players. My husband and I check the cabins and then stroll the deck under a canopy of velvet black sky hung with luminous globes of stars. We give ourselves over to the beautiful night, the balmy breeze, and our togetherness. We draw our deck chairs close together and whisper a few sweet nothings to one another as we speak of the new direction of our lives.

At this moment we hear Barbara screaming, sailors running, and iron ladders being scaled; lanterns and lights of every port appear. Little Susan is not in her bed! I run to the deck, where the children had played that afternoon. Not there. Some sailors are descending from ladders alongside the ship with long-beam flashlights to check the waves. A lifetime goes by, with only the voices of Barbara and Bill calling their child's name.

And then . . . from the very height of the ship, we hear Barbara sobbing and laughing hysterically. The doors to the shaft that leads down to the engine room had been left open to carry off the odors of heavy oil and to cool the shaft. At its very edge, little Susan is kneeling and looking down into the pit. Her shadow is reflected on the open door by a reddish light as Barbara scoops her way to safety. How did she get there? How did she manage the ladders? We'll never know.

Granddad's Workshop

By Henry Gray

A little while ago I started to prepare a story that I called "Tales my father told me." It turned out that there were fewer tales than I thought. As I began to get into the stories they inevitably segued to my granddad instead, for reasons that shortly will become apparent. I therefore decided to title this piece as above, in memory of the workshop and of the rubber stamp with exactly that name on it, which Granny had made so Granddad could mark the pieces he had crafted. Many of these have come down in the family; others became spread among the many friends that Granddad had in Terre Haute.

If I go way back, to about the time when I began to pick up tools and use them, I can remember a rudimentary truck that I built using things at hand. Among these were some beautiful brass gears, very nicely cut, that were loose on some of the shelves in our garage at Allendate, and which I used for the wheels. I was using the truck to "haul" weeds that I was supposed to be removing from our vegetable garden. I was not enthusiastic about that job and this stratagem interfered with my assigned work, much to my satisfaction and to my mother's annoyance.

I think Dad was upset seeing those beautiful and expensive gears misused. They were parts from what had been a wonderful model locomotive, an electric prototype, about 18 inches long, which had come to me at Christmas a few years before. Dad had built it to exact scale—which meant that he had to build the track, which also was a beautiful job. Wooden ties, third rail to the side, not down the middle as in those Lionel things. It had only a few feet of track, and no cars to haul, but Dad pronounced it too weak and dismantled it, intending to add a second electric motor. I saw it run only once, and it was never rebuilt. Nor are there any photographs.

"Let's fix this," Dad proclaimed, and picking up my truck he hiked across the bridge to Granddad's place and entered the workshop, where he promptly dismantled my masterpiece and built another, while I watched. The wheels were segments of logs, and a pivoting front axle could be steered by cords that went up and around a spool that served as a steering wheel. It was a nice piece of semi-rustic craftsmanship, but it wasn't mine, and I promptly lost interest.

Soon, however, I began to build things that were then called pushmobiles. My work on them was, I think, to some extend inspired by the beginnings of the Soap Box Derby, the details of which we could read about in the paper and hear first-hand on the radio. I think they also appeared in the newsreels at our local theaters. These events were supposed to encourage boys to enter the field of engineering.

I think my first pushmobile was an unstable box mounted on a steel-bodied wagon that had the usual tongue for pulling. But I wanted a carefree-like vehicle suitable for coasting down the hills near our home. I collected some sets of wheels and with a big wooden box as a body I got well along until I came to the question of steering. Somewhere I had found an antique wood-rim steering wheel, but I was stymied. Granddad, who as usual, was watching from another corner of his workshop while I worked, came to my rescue. With a piece of broomstick and a length of steel cable, together we fashioned a simple but functional steering apparatus. This was Granddad's *modus operandi*. He would watch me struggle, make mistakes, and then offer the minimum assistance I needed to get my project on the way again.

Earlier Granddad had given my sister Caroline and me pedal cars. She was so young she could hardly pedal hers, but he wanted to treat both of us, his only grandchildren, equally. My car was a fancy one—a Marmon, no less, with a windshield that lowered (for more speed), a crank horn, black fenders, and a greenish-gray body. I loved it, but it had two flaws: first, as a pedal car it did not coast well, and when we moved to our suburban home, which had no sidewalks, it did not go as fast as I wished, and second, I outgrew it.

I think I solved the first problem by simply removing the pedal assembly. But to move the seat back, to allow for my lengthening legs, I had to remove the rear deck. I have wondered how Granddad felt as he saw his expensive gift disintegrate, but he said nothing. I got heavier and the rear springs (there were none in front) sagged, so I moved them so they could accommodate my greater bulk. Then after seeing some of the elaborate mechanisms that were then allowed on Soap-Box Derby cars, I took off the front axle assembly and installed springs and levers that could act somewhat the same as the knee-action independent front suspension of the mid-thirties cars. I had a good imagination! Eventually, the entire pedal car was trashed except the front and rear axles.

I think this is the end of the pushmobile saga. I do not remember having built others. Still, I had other projects: radio and speaker cabinets, for example, and construction and repair of radios and amplifiers for phonographs. As usual, Granddad was nearby, ready to help if needed. A skilled surgeon, he was also a craftsman in wood. And I think there is a moral to this story, or maybe two or three.

But I should go on, as I have no described his wonderful shop. Granddad was always handy with tools, often repaired on the road his cars that began in 1902 with a one-cylinder Oldsmobile buckboard. This could lead to another story, but I must get back to the workshop. The workshop began with an extensive set of antique hand tools that came with the Grown County cottage that he once owned. These were moved to Terre Haute when the cabin was sold, and they formed the nucleus of the shop that occupied part of the garage that was built to go with my grandparents new summer abode, which came to be known as "The Dingle." About this time Granddad's doctor again advised him to learn to unwind from his stressful profession. One suggestion was to get more into woodworking in his shop.

Which power tool came first, I don't recall, but eventually he accumulated several. A table saw, a belt-disc sander, and a jigsaw, on which my dad made dozens of wonderful puzzles, then a big fad. A jointer, shaper, and a lathe were added. From Brown County also came a set of tobacco boxes that held nuts, bolts, nails, and other needs. It was a wonderfully functional shop, and I used it frequently. Working in the shop I learned another lesson. If Granddad found his tools out of place, I was locked out of the shop for a week or two. That lesson still sticks with me. Even though my workbench becomes a mess, my tools are where they belong.

Eventually, Granddad and Grandmother found their country house too much of a burden, sold it, and moved to town. Granddad kept most of the antique hand tools, but neither Dad nor I had room for the power tools. The new owner of the house was happy to buy them along with the house. In their new home in town, Granddad had a small room for his workshop and bought a multipurpose power tool, a Shopsmith, which could be converted to a lathe, drill press, or sander. But his eyes failed rapidly—he had glaucoma—and he did not use his new shop much. He died about the time we moved to Bloomington, and his Shopsmith became the nucleus of my own worship, where I applied much of what I had learned from him, years before. ✳

Barbara Restle

Bom Dia Gringa! (Good Morning, Foreigner!)

By Rosemary Messick

Dawn comes early when you live in Brazil, fifteen degrees south of the equator. The city of Maceio sprawls along the lagoons that flow into the Atlantic. The city of nearly one million is the capitol of Alagoas (lagoons) state. These calm turquoise waters were one of the city's main attractions for me. Swimming is good nearly all year in the warm, shallow reef-protected bays, but not in the lagoons as they are more polluted. To take advantage of these conditions, swimmers must rise early and seek shelter before the sun reaches 45 degrees above the horizon, which happens at about eight in the morning.

I lived in a high rise across the palm-lined boulevard from the bay. My mornings began with a swim. I had a morning routine: I walked across the five lanes of traffic, and prepared with a full coating of sunscreen and further protected by a long-sleeved tee-shirt over my stretched-out swimsuit and topped off by an old baseball cap to protect my evermore apparent scalp. Walking in flip-flops, I carried the rest of my gear of goggles and ear plugs to prevent further chronic tinnitus, or surfer's ear, resulting from too much swimming. This outfit and gear marked me as eccentric and probably *Gringa*. Clearly, I was not a local. Brazilian women go to the beach not to swim, but to tan. They enter the water only to cool off. They are a style show. They leave a perfumed trail, have carefully maintained manicures and pedicures and protect their perfect make-up by wearing large beach hats. Their outfits include upscale beach sandals, the latest 'dental floss' bikini, topped off with, but not obscured by, a colorful beach sarong, which had probably been handmade by local lace makers according to the wearer's specifications.

Maneuvering the rush hour traffic, I headed for the handsome copper-skinned local, Roosevelt, pronounced "Hosevelte," who would be setting up his green coconut business. Twenty year-old Hosevelte must arrive early seven days a week to protect his selling place. As I was a steady customer, Hosevelte was glad to do me the favor of guarding my flip-flops while I swam. Before I made his acquaintance and became his customer, several pairs of flip-flops I left on the beach had walked away while I was in the water.

Hosevelte always had a large smile and greeting, *"Como vai minha Senhora? Tudo bom?"* (How is my lady? Everything O.K.?) And I responded with the anticipated, *"Sim, tudo bom. E como esta o Senhor?"* (Yes, all's well. And how is the Mister?) Whatever his true situation, he was always fine. I feel he wouldn't have been if I had not responded with my part of the scripted ritual of respect.

With our exchange completed, he resumed chopping tops off the coconut husks with his machete and putting them to cool in his Styrofoam boxes. His operation was almost totally portable—beach umbrella, machete, Styrofoam boxes and a packet of straws. He depended on daily deliveries of chipped ice and green coconuts and daily garbage pickup by the city. (Beaches are the prime tourist attraction and get special attention with daily raking.) He called for additional ice or coconuts from his cellular phone when business was good. Hosevelte eked out a living tending his trade in good weather, and defending his territory on rainy days. He arrived early and stayed until eleven in the evening.

I left my flip-flops in the shade of the coconut palms, gingerly treading across the shell-strewn, already warm sand toward the water's edge. As usual, I was the last to arrive at the gathering spot. My arrival was greeted, *"Bom dia Grinda! Esta sabendo do ultimo do seu presidente?"* Good morning, *Gringa*! Do you know the latest of your President?) Much earlier I had concluded that Gringa was a term of endearment in this context. I listened as Gilberto, Dr. Gustavo, Pedro and Fernando related their version of "W's" latest "bad" act. They waited for my reaction. From long experience, I interpreted this baiting as their way to level the verbal playing field and relieve the inferiority complex they felt around Americans. It offered me inclusion into their custom of belittling and deprecating Brazilian politicians. I responded, *"Neo e incrivel?"* ("Isn't it incredible?") Sometimes I stirred up something salty that I had gleaned from reading the previous day's newspaper, *Folba de Sao Paulo*, into the morning fat-chewing. I "subscribed" to *The New York Times* of Brazil at my local espresso bar after *siesta* each afternoon. The *Folba* arrived on the noon flight from the south and was expensive. Locals listened to the national newscast or read the *Gazetta's* version of events. Owned by the family of Brazil's impeached President Collor, the word was that the only fact one could trust in the *Gazetta* was the report of yesterday's temperature . . . and even it needed to be double-checked.

After conversation waned, someone often commented, "Rose, (pronounced Hose), *voce e a Gringa mais brasileira que ja conbeci!"* ("Rose, you are the most Brazilian *Gringa* I've known!") And I was flattered.

Then we spent some moments trading jokes. Usually these jokes compared nationalities. And always Brazilians came out on top due to all manner of deviousness. Gilberto is the owner of a beach-front hotel. He is a blue-eyed, freckle-faced Portuguese. He eyed the sun creeping upward and said it's time for him to get going. He waded out into deeper water and swam west in what I thought of as his Portuguese Waterdog stroke. It involved lots of dolphin-like dipping and vigorous splashing of arms and legs. Then the bona-fide long distance swimmers, Doctor Gustavo and his younger companion Pedro, walked further east where they could strike out to deeper water and could swim maintaining their rhythmic Australian crawl to where the fishing boats are anchored about 500 meters west. Nando, the eldest of our group swam and rested his way westward near the beach, and I entered last.

I swam in a different direction. Since I didn't want to walk back along the hot sand, I swam south, perpendicular to the coast. Wading to where my feet no longer touched bottom, I put on my goggles and plugs and began my own dog paddle version of breast stroke and side stroke. A restful combination which allowed me to alternately observe the bottom and the receding shoreline. I collected drifting plastics, stuffing them down the front of my suit. Later, I deposited them in garbage cans. I saw small sergeant majors, their yellow-white stripes glinting through a sunlit wave. Approaching the coral I dived to see if the wrasses (colorful fish) were visible in the crevasse they back into for protection. It's rare to see other fish. Local fishermen catch and eat anything that moves. Sea urchins have taken over large dead coral expanses. I swam in a cemetery of marine life.

After about twenty minutes, I turned toward the shore. Not counting strokes, I let my body work while I put world events and the evidence of ecological destruction surrounding me out of my mind. Mentally, I made a list of what pleased me about these moments: the warm, turquoise water, the reef that protects this bay from sharks, the constancy of the semi-tropical climate, the niche I had created in this culture, the health and peace these mornings provided by body and spirit. This was my mantra. This special moment left me in an endorphin high. As I approached the shallow water I began to anticipate the cup of steaming coffee I would soon enjoy. ✳

If Fish Could Talk

By Bob Webb (Webboe)

"Why are you called O Great Walleye of Gull Rock?" asked one of the younger fingerlings in the school.

"It is the name given me by the walleye hunters from the south who want me for a trophy to hang on their wall," replied the older, wiser lunker. "I will tell you a little about them so you can be more wary and not be caught.

"I have learned much about the hunter by observing a group from Bloomington, Indiana; Curry, Moore, Martin, and McDaniel appear to be the regulars and

McDonald, Chitwood, Lynch and Webb make the trip every other year or so. About the first of June each year a shiny station wagon pulling a trailer laden with gear crests the hill at the J & J Resort to signal two weeks of the hunt. They always travel in a wagon marked BUICK because the one called Curry sells this make of car back in Bloomington. I'm told the entire crew drives Buicks sold to them by Curry."

Little Wally Walleye interrupted at this point. "You mean they all live together, sleep together, hunt together for years and years and Curry the Car Man takes money from the other hunters just to drive his cars?"

"I'm afraid so," Wally replied "OMG and to think they call us fish!" The rocks echoed with their laughter.

"How have you learned so much about these hunters, O Wise One?" gurgled Wally.

"I have talked to many cast-offs who have traveled all over Gull Rock with the hunters only to be rejected because they were not 'tender as Moore's heart' or big enough to take back to Indiana—dead—frozen—whose stories have told me much about these hunters.

"Let me warn you they are very serious about the hunt. Months before the trip, meetings are held where they boast of previous years' catches, show slides of Gull Rock, drink beer, tell jokes and develop a plan for the next trip. Do you realize it is harder to crack this little society of walleye hunters than to join a church? And no wonder—just listen to some of the requirements.

1. Buick ownership.
2. Skill at filleting a walleye, or
3. Ability at KP (subject to scrutiny of Martin) or
4. Some culinary talent.

Since 2 and 4 are usually assigned long before the trip, any newcomers (less than eight-year members) had better be good at 3.

5. Ability to tell a joke or to laugh at a joke even if you've heard it before.
6. Willingness to endure stress during the 28-hour ride to and from Gull Rock
7. Be able to see humor in adversity.
8. And last, but most importantly, be able to take advice on whatever you're doing, from all the others. On fire building, for example:

Martin, get the pliers, the coffee's perkin',

Barbara Restle

Spread it out more—we've got enough coals,
Here, try this stuff we used in the army—works every time, Better move the coffee pot.

"You see, my children, the ways of the hunter are strange indeed. How can I prepare you to defend yourselves against creatures who will sit all day in a boat in the rain, sleet, snow, fighting the wind and waves, suffering from chapped lips, sore butts, aching backs, and bruised kidneys, contending with a malfunctioning motor-usually the one called Old Red Rooster—and then come in at the end of the day say "Isn't this a great life?'

I well remember the 1975 invasion of Gull Rock. For two weeks a group of your elders followed the hunters to study their behavior patterns and hunting techniques. Pay attention for you are big enough to be the prey of these men.

The one called McDaniel employs scientific methods in search and capture. He studies charts, reads books, checks the moon, the water temperature, the color of the rocks, the thickness of the moss on the trees, the wind direction, the barometric pressure, then uses this vast store house of knowledge to hunt at the same time, same place with the same bait as all of the others.

"You will have no problem recognizing the mild-mannered easygoing Chitwood. But don't be fooled by demeanor for he is a hustler, long on experience; he will swoop you right into the boat. Now, if you want to have some fun, wait till he is told to get a beer for his partner and when he lays down his pole, just tug on his line. You'll get rig, line, pole and reel . . . . splat, down it goes in front of your nose to the bottom of Gull Rock Lake . . . score one for the walleye! This causes a commotion topside and you will end up with a trophy to hang on your favorite rock.

"Do watch out for the one called McDonald, the mouthpiece for the mob. If you aren't careful he will talk you right into the net. He even talks in his sleep—so say those who should know. His method for the hunt is simple; he goes early, stays late and throws everything he has at us. You just watch his line—I don't mean that lawyer talk—I mean the end of his fishing line.

"Among the hunters is a high ranking U.S. Army Officer, Lt. Col. H.M. Lynch who has served with distinction. In tribute to such a distinguished career, the hunters demonstrate their great esteem by assigning Lynch to kitchen cleaning detail. Lynch is best known for being prepared for almost any eventuality during the hunt. If it rains during shore lunch, he has a protective cover for the fire (and seven companions to tell him how to string it up). His most popular contribution to the welfare of the group is his boat coffee. Lynch claims his special brew will cure frostbite, snake bite, low flying crop dusters, duck disease, athletes foot and a host of maladies yet unproven. Lynch is the one who caught Fat Agnes several years ago, your Northern cousin who weighed in at 17 pounds.

"Which brings us to the Great Hunter himself, the Godfather of the Bloomington mob, Bob the Butcher Moore." Hearing the name, all the walleyes gathered around and began to hiss and boo. It is no small task for a walleye to hiss. The water erupted with bubbles all around. "You see, Moore has an uncanny sense of detecting our feeding and hiding places. Once there he gives full concentration to catching walleye, mainly

me. I can't relax for a second while he is on the water because he doesn't relax for a second. He works at it, changing speed, direction, hook size, sharpening his hook, changing leader length, busy, busy, busy. Moore, the relentless hunter. Don't try to suck a minnow off his hook or you are his dinner. This guy can feel where your mouth is in relation to that enormous hook. We must not judge him too harshly. He only keeps enough for eating, the legal limit for take-home, some for the camp hostess and a few for strangers on the lake down on their luck.

"Webboe is no threat to our kind. He spends much of his time laboring over a hot stove preparing special recipes or apple pie. And when he is on the lake he is busy quarreling with Old Red Rooster, the outboard engine, or snagging sunken logs and big boulders, or netting other hunters' catches or fetching them a minnow or stringing their catch, or opening a beer for his buddy. In this way, I believe this hunter is a friend of the walleye. There is no cause to fear him. Chances are if caught by Webboe he will admire your beauty, maybe even hug you to his breast and then return you to your home in the black depths of Gull Rock.

"You have heard the story of how to avoid capture. I know my time will soon be up and this may be the year that you must carry on in my place. But then, I wouldn't mind being immortalized on a wall in Bloomington, Indiana." ⁂

Slug: A Dog of the Sixties

By Walter Taylor

In was 1968. There was a really bad war. Martin Luther King and Robert Kennedy were killed and the drug scene was just hitting the Baby Boomers. And Slug was born on a cushion on the back porch while the children, Baby Boomers all, watched.

Everything about Slug seemed to have taken the wrong turn at the genetic fork in the road. He had his mother's Sheltie hair and orange and white coloring and his Pug father's heavy shoulders and neck muscles. His short-nosed, wall-eyed half-Pug face had the appearance of a hairy, smashed Jack-O'Lantern, his left eye trailing off on one side, his tongue hanging out the other.

Slug's obedience training, which fell to the kids, was a catastrophe. He would come if you called him, usually. He barely understood "STAY." I cannot imagine Slug coming to heel. He was potty trained enough so that he could come indoors for short times—if you watched him. In a true sense he was wild. And from the start, there was a major problem with Slug: a serious over-supply of testosterone.

He was the most territorial creature I ever encountered. He hated all garbage men and they came into the yard with trepidation. Once he chased a salesman, a former Green Bay running back, right out of the yard. Our neighbors had a skittish maid and as soon as Slug smelled fear, she was a prisoner in the laundry room. Slug himself was absolutely fearless. He put our neighbor's mean-spirited mutt on his back in a breath. I have seen him stand his ground while a skunk squirted him in the face. A four-foot rattlesnake bit him in the forehead and he lived.

It developed into a kind of game. Slug getting into trouble, me getting him out of it. Not satisfied with his own territory, he had to visit others'. No fence would hold him. He would be gone two days, three days—always back just before I gave him up for dead. Filthy, sometimes bloody, back to civilization from a world of love and war and canine adventure I could never understand. Somehow I loved him for all that.

We moved perilously close to co-dependency. We had moved to a home near the Rio Grande and Slug decided to take a swim. Then he found he couldn't get himself out. I had to step into the water to get him. I sometimes took Slug for a run with me on the levee but it never worked. Just when I thought he was ready to fall in step, I'd see him halfway across a cotton field, a desperate jackrabbit bobbing along ahead of him. At these times when I would catch him I would always get a certain sheepish look, innocent of all repentance.

Look what I did, master. I ran away but you came and got me!

Slug kept trying to tell me about that mysterious world that he would run away to, about enjoying his nights of love and war before returning spent and ready to be taken care of. A world that humans realize—when we think about it—must be there, but one which we can never know. And so the boundary between me and Slug defines my limits and the limits of my kind.

The Sixties, finally morphed into the Eighties. The Boomers were getting gray and Slug was nearly fifteen. His back was stiff with old age and the vet had already removed two tumors. It was time to do what I always knew I would have to do.

I took Slug for a last walk along the levee. We had gone about a quarter of a mile—and suddenly he was off in the cotton field, heading for the fence. When I caught him on the far side of the field, he was panting and salivating and looking sheepish. *You came for me, master. You always do.*

Our last little game.

I took my companion of fifteen years to the vet's, signed the euthanasia papers and went with my wife on a planned trip to Santa Fe.

And when I got back, I went for a run along the levee. It was a fine spring morning, the panorama of the Franklin Mountains and the Rio Grande valley spread out before me. I passed the spot where Slug had made his last bolt for freedom. At that point, a dog I had never seen before appeared; a female. She did not look at me, but fell in step with me, moving easily along the levee at my heel. This dog's hair was Sheltie length and she had the Sheltie's orange and white coloring, an old dog, her back stiff. She looked exactly like a large female Slug.

We ran for a half mile like that and then, still without looking at me, the dog turned and moved off down a side path.

I am not given to hallucinations—not, at least, since the Sixties. I merely report that the first time I went running after Slug died, this dog that looked like Slug appeared and ran with me along the canal. I had never seen this dog before and I have never seen this dog since.

*
**

Barbara Restle

My Two Goats

By Bernard Clayton

To celebrate my 90th birthday, my family gave me a milk goat.

I can't keep her on the Meadowood campus, so it is being cared for by a poor family in a small village in Kenya, Africa. From time to time I hope to hear how well she is doing producing milk and income for the family, and what I can do to help her upbringing. This all was possible with the help of World Vision.

I have always loved goats and once upon a time I had a billy-goat with long curving horns. I was six years old.

I discovered this goat in a barnyard at the edge of a small town in northern Indiana where my father published a weekly newspaper. I looked at the goat and knew that I could harness him to my red wagon and carry groceries home from the store and my father's newspapers to the post office. The possibilities of what I could do with the goat seemed endless.

The man who bought and sold farm animals said, yes, he would sell me the goat for 50 cents. I am not proud of what I did to get the 50 cents. I took it from a dish of coins my mother kept in the kitchen. Two quarters. I did not ask. I just took the money.

I led the goat home and put him in a small shed in the backyard, not telling my parents that their son just bought a goat. But I did have a goat. Actually, it was a nasty looking old billy-goat with dirty hair and a powerful

smell of a creature that had not had a bath for a long, long, time. About then I got scared.

To kill time to think about it, I climbed a maple tree in the front yard and decided to stay there until I found an answer. By then it was dark. I heard my mother call me to come home from wherever I was and my father got in his car and drove around the neighborhood searching for me.

My father looked around our house and opened the door to the shed. I could hear him cry out to my mother, "Good Lord, there's a goat in our shed."

From my place in the tree I could see the town marshal drive up to the house to offer help finding me. I was not only scared, but cold and hungry. The goat in the shed was warmer. It was getting out of hand. I decided I should let them know where I was.

I took off a shoe and threw it at a distance against the front door. It hit with a bang and a clatter that brought my father and the town marshal with flashlights to the foot of my tree. The town marshal, with a big star on his chest and a huge revolver at his hip, gave me a long lecture about buying a goat with money that wasn't mine. He implied that a small boy could go to jail for the rest of his life.

But there was still the goat in the shed. I had great hopes that I could harness him to my wagon. But the goat just stood and looked at me as if I was crazy. He was old and set in his ways and wasn't about to become a beast of burden. Nor did I want to be downwind for he smelled to high heaven. He wasn't a mean goat, but he wasn't friendly either. He was just an old billy goat that had been around for a long time. He was not worth 50 cents.

My father let me have the goat for most of the next day and then he marched me and the old goat back to the farmer in the barn to return the goat. The farmer gave the 50 cents back when my father hinted he might write an editorial in the paper about hornswoggling a juvenile, and a very young one at that.

It would be 84 years before I got my second goat.

*
**

Pink Bloomers

By Richard P. Letsinger

I was born in the year 1921 and am fortunate to remember many things during the mid-1920's. My mother and father were both about forty years old when my twin brother and I were born on July 31, 1921.

Mother was not into the fast-moving pace of the post-World War I days of the early 1920's, although she had her long hair bobbed and wore it short like the flappers of the era. She consented to some of the styles for shorter dresses than she had never before worn in her lifetime. While dresses were short, with hems above bare or silk stockinged knees, her dresses were modest. Under things were carefully planned.

As a small boy, however, I was somehow aware that mother had pink silk bloomers of ample size and they reached just above her knees. I would sometimes catch a glimpse of them and be curious as to their usefulness.

Whenever we went someplace for an overnight visit or trip, mother always would comment that she needed some extra under things in case she might be in an accident and would need fresh replacement bloomers.

My older brother was graduating from DePauw University and all of us planned to spend the weekend at Greencastle, Indiana, for this outstanding event. He was an honor student and a Delta Upsilon fraternity man. Our sister had also been a DePauw person and my parents were in the class of 1904. It was an important event for our family.

It was a hot June day when we packed to leave for Greencastle. In those days, a boy would have only one suit for all seasons and Bob, my twin, and I had wooly knickers and stockings to wear. I hated the hot wool on my skin and those wooly knickers made me feel itchy all the time. I wanted to scratch myself a lot. Mother felt sorry for me and made a wonderful suggestion. She asked me to try on a pair of her pink silk bloomers and told me to wear them under my wooly knickers.

This was a wonderful solution and, while I was pretty self conscious about wearing pink bloomers, I was assured no one would know the difference. The comfort of keeping the wool off my skin was so nice, I felt reassured and happy wearing mother's pink silk bloomers. To keep Bob's mouth shut about this was another matter to be handled later, I thought.

We arrived in Greencastle and got settled, then visited John's fraternity house where we met some of his good fraternity friends. The outstanding moment of that day was when older brother John invited Bob, Betty, my younger sister, and me to go with him to the local airfield for an airplane ride.

These planes were of World War I vintage with an open cockpit and two sets of wings. In the front cockpit sat the pilot and behind was one seat for a passenger. These were old-fashioned "barnstorming" pilots making a living from their war pilot days by offering plane rides. It was thrilling to think of going for an airplane ride, though scary!

Getting permission from our parents never entered my mind. So brother John bought us a ticket apiece for a plane ride. I remember so vividly how it felt climbing on the lower wing and getting fastened by a belt to hold me in the open cockpit. With a whoooooooosh, we went plummeting down the grassy runway away from a barn and down an open field, and then slowly zoomed over some trees and away into the sky. The air rushed past my head and the breeze was fast and thrilling. In this open cockpit it was easy to see the wonderful landscape rush below our plane.

After about ten thrilling minutes in the open sky, we began a descent and finally bumped to a rather rough stop. My brothers and sister ran to the plane as I got up, unfastened my seatbelt and stepped onto the wing and then the ground.

But when I hopped off the wing of the plane, I felt and heard a ripping sound. I had caught my knickers on something beside the seat and a big rip opened up on the leg of my knickers, exposing mother's pink bloomers. I was mortified and embarrassed as my siblings laughed at my plight. I grabbed the open tear and held it tightly together so no one else around would see my pink bloomers!

My dear blessed mother saw my embarrassment when we met her later, and she supplied me with a big safety pin to hold the ragged pants together.

But never would I forget her good advice to pack that extra pair of necessities so important in case of accident . . . especially those pink bloomers.

Richard P. Letsinger is a retired realtor and an Army veteran of the European Theatre in World War II. He divides his time between residences at Meadowood and Singer Island, Florida.

Barbara Restle

Take a Bus

By Olimpia Barbera
[As told to Barbara Restle]

I had not lived at Meadowood very long when I experienced a memorable evening that not only left me soaking wet while wearing a formal evening gown, but also found me chauffeured around Bloomington at midnight in a pizza truck.

The adventure filled evening began innocently, with Mary, who was my neighbor, suggesting that the two of us go together to a performance of an opera production at IU. Mary explained that she preferred driving us herself rather than taking the Meadowood bus. The evening of the opera we drove to the Musical Arts Center (MAC) where we parked in the large parking lot, and walked across the street to the MAC. We thoroughly enjoyed the opera.

After the opera, we found a torrential rain in progress. Mary told me that it was not necessary for both of us to get soaking wet and told me to wait a few minutes, and then walk to the corner of the driveway on Jordan where she would pick me up.

I walked to the corner in the rain and in a few minutes Mary drives up and as I tried to get into the front door of the car, I found it locked. Mary could not figure out how to unlock the door and as I and my formal gown were now drenched I decided to get into the back seat which fortunately was unlocked.

We drove in a hard rain without the windshield wipers. From the back seat I asked Mary to turn on the windshield wipers so she could see where she was going. By this time I figured we had driven about three blocks and I could not see street signs. I couldn't see anything and I knew Mary couldn't see anything either. Mary said she couldn't figure out how to turn the windshield wipers on. It was true that the inside of the car was very dark and there was no way I could help her. However, her next remark was quite alarming.

"Olimpia, I have lived in Bloomington for 35 years and tonight I do not know where I am." I myself was a new resident in Bloomington and I knew, that on a rainy night, I also would not be able to find my way home to Meadowood. However, Mary had lived here for 35 years and I felt she should know her way home, she should be able to figure out how to turn on the wipers and she should have known how to unlock the front door of her car.

"Mary, I see a pizza place down the street. Let me go in and ask directions." Mary agreed that this appeared to be the best move to make. Perhaps someone inside could advise us how to get home. Mary parked in a parking lot and I got out of the back seat and went into the restaurant feeling relieved that we had made a good decision. I left my handbag in the back seat.

The man behind the counter looked at me in my wet formal evening outfit and said he could come out and turn on the wipers. However, I would have to wait a few minutes while he finished serving a customer. When the man and I came out into the parking lot, we found no car and no Mary. I was embarrassed and did not know what this good man must be thinking of me. I was at a complete loss to explain why Mary and the car had disappeared into the rainy night.

The man explained that he was the manager of the pizza parlor and that he would like to help me get home. He asked me where I lived. I told him and he said he did not know where Meadowood was and that he had only recently arrived from Chicago. The only directions I could think of was driving north on Walnut and then turning onto 46. I climbed into his pizza delivery truck and I was immediately aware of the strong aromas of anchovy, salami, and a half dozen cheeses cloyingly attaching to my wet formal gown.

We finally find our way to Meadowood and I guided my chauffeur to Mary's house so I can retrieve my handbag with the key to my front door. I knock on her door and there is no answer. It was now well after midnight. My pizza chauffeur then knocks on the door really hard and there is finally a response. Mary's husband had been sound asleep and was puzzled as to why I am at the front door with a strange man and not his wife, Mary. I ask for my handbag with my door key inside and he answers that Mary is not home. This is alarming news for all of us. Where is she? And why did she leave me inside the pizza parlor?

My chauffeur, patient man that he is, drove me to the Health Pavilion where we finally were helped and told to wait a few minutes until one of the maintenance men could help us. When the maintenance man arrives he said he would drive me to my house and open my door. I replied that my chauffeur would be happy to drive me, and all I needed was a key. The maintenance man answered that it was against regulations to permit me to go

to my home with a man not recognized by a staff member of Meadowood. The manager of the pizza parlor looked embarrassed at the suggestion that the two of us had anything in mind other than getting me home and out of the rain. I embraced him fleetingly and thanked him for all his help.

About one o'clock I was gratefully out of my wet and pizza—smelling clothes when the phone rang. It was Mary. She apologized many times and said the police drove her home. I was too tired to continue the conversation and suggested we talk again at some other time.

The next day Mary brought me a lovely bouquet of flowers and made every attempt to explain leaving me at the pizza parlor. I asked her a question that needed an answer. "Why did you leave me?" Mary answered, "I asked you several questions and you did not answer." I responded, "Well, I wasn't in the back seat." Mary responded again, "Well, you never answered."

It was not necessary to ask any more questions. I said to Mary, "This will be our secret." I wanted to respect her.

With this experience in mind, I leave you with one message: TAKE A BUS!

Ups and Downs

By Elizabeth Droege

Once upon a time, back when commercial flying was fun, I worked for United Airlines. Back then, United was still using some small Douglas airplanes, DC-3s. The cabins of these planes were not pressurized and when we had to work hard and fast, when our altitude was higher than usual, we sometimes sucked on little oxygen pipes back in the galley. I loved those planes, loved them because we were not above the weather, but in it, like boats on water, sometimes turbulent, sometimes smooth.

A note about terminology: I was a stewardess, not a flight attendant. Only women worked United's flights in those days. That was true of almost all United

States airlines. Eastern was the notable exception: Eastern hired men and called them stewards.

There was room in a DC-3 for a pilot, a co-pilot, a stewardess, and twenty-one passengers, all in comfortable seats with plenty of leg room. Unless the weather was really terrible, no mealtime passed without a full meal. First-class passage had not been introduced because all our passengers were first-class.

It was illegal, back then, to serve alcoholic beverages on U.S. airline flights. As a matter of fact, people were cautioned not to drink much before boarding because the cabins were not pressurized. Passenger agents were told not to board anyone who

reeked of alcohol. Not every agent would abide by those rules, of course.

I remember working a night flight that stopped in South Bend to pick up fifteen Notre Dame Alumni who had been celebrating their homecoming victory. The South Bend passenger agent warned me before he boarded them explaining that fifteen of the twenty-one seats was way over half the payload. "Besides," he told me, "those fifteen guys could easily beat me bloody."

The noisiest of these men told me that he had his own plane at Midway in Chicago. Ten minutes later he was sound asleep, but not before he had invited me to fly to Paris with most of them that very night. "A little nap," he said, "and I'll be ready to go. You could come along and serve snacks and drinks." I thought not.

When we landed, at least half a dozen women were out there on the tarmac to meet their husbands. Since I heard nothing later about an over-the-ocean disaster, I assumed that these wives got the last word and it was not "Have a nice trip."

What you just read is a "There we were at ten thousand feet . . ." yarn. Almost all retired airline people keep a collection of these in mind for the rest of their lives. Some of us tell them at the slightest provocation.

The next story is one of my favorites. One cold day about a week before Christmas, Bob Hope and his agent joined my westbound flight to Denver. They were allowed to board before the other passengers and sat in 1A and 1B. Bob next to the window, his agent was quite clear about their wanting to be undisturbed. We were trained to respect that.

This was a "puddle-jumper" trip, up and down at Cedar Rapids, Des Moines, Lincoln, Grand Island, North Platte and finally Denver. I served lunch as soon as we reached cruising altitude. Bob smiled and thanked me when I brought his tray and thanked me again later when I picked it up. "Thanks," he said.

"Thanks," I say to myself as I carry trays back to the galley. Thanks. The great Bob Hope, the comic who kept our troops in stitches and what I get is "Thanks." Oh, well, he's not here to entertain me, he's here on the way to Denver. Oh, well . . .

As we traveled west, the weather gradually got worse. Shortly before we got to North Platte, George, our co-pilot, came back to the cabin and announced that we would have to deplane once we landed. There would be a delay. He was willing to field a few question. Would we be very late getting to Denver? "Probably". Would we leave for Denver at all? "Certainly hoped so". Was there engine trouble? "Absolutely not, just weather trouble".

"And if you have questions later about possible accommodations in North Platte", he concluded, with a wicked smile in my direction, "Liz will know what to do. But right now I'm expecting all of you, including her, to keep your seat belts fastened."

When we landed at North Platte, we were taken to a separate room off the concourse while the two pilots went off to study weather maps and talk to air traffic controllers. Bob Hope disappeared as well. It is up to me to keep an eye on this nervous, unhappy little group of people. I talked one of the passenger agents into bringing us cookies, juice and coffee. That helped a little. But there was no way I could answer the crucial question: would we leave North Platte and get to Denver today?

A well-dressed business type looked up from the papers in his briefcase to tell me in no uncertain terms that next time he'd fly American Airlines. Fine with me, I thought. Not the sort of thing I could possibly say, of course, and keep my job! Another passenger responded quickly, "You think American never runs into bad weather?" I offered to get them both another cup of coffee.

A middle-aged woman was still clutching a basketball she'd carried onto the plane. "A Christmas present for my grandson," she said. "Oh I do hope we'll get to Denver tonight," she told me. "I've never stayed anywhere in this town."

I assured her that should we have to stay in North Platte, we'd find her a hotel room. That was a given. Paid customers did not have to sleep in airports, not then. United would pick up the tab.

A tired, sulky teenager had been giving his mother fits ever since they got on at Lincoln. He was not happy about having to spend Christmas with his father. "Hey, Miss, my Dad will be waiting at the airport in Denver. If it turns out we're not getting to Denver, how will he know? He'll be so upset if he gets out there . . ."

"If he phones the airport, he'll know," I told the boy, but we both knew that might not happen.

When a door behind me opened, I turned, hoping to see George bringing news. No, not George, it was Bob Hope, and he greeted us all with a big smile. "You were thinking maybe I was Santa Claus?" he asked.

He headed straight for the basketball. "Mind if I check the bounce on this thing?" he asked. Of course Grandma didn't mind. She was speechless with delight as Bob dribbled the ball back and forth in front of his small audience, asking them questions, coming up with hilarious answers, turning bad news into fun.

I can't recreate the comedy—I don't remember the lines. All I know is that when we left North Platt, I had nineteen happy passengers on board. Bob had said goodbye. He and his agent had decided to stay in North Platte: post-performance fatigue, perhaps.

Dear Bob, thanks for the memory. ✸

The beloved Douglas DC-3 flown by United Airlines

Do Not Play The F-Sharp Key Too Much

By Joseph Rezits

If one has prepared thoroughly for a recital or concert performance, one can usually count on a certain degree of predictability. Of course there are many variables, such as the state of one's "nerves," acoustic properties of the hall, the response of the audience, and for pianists, the challenge of using different instruments for different occasions. However, above and beyond the above, there are sometimes bizarre, totally unexpected elements that turn an otherwise "normal" performance into an adventure.

On the 11th of January, 1950, I had the good fortune to appear as soloist with the Philadelphia Orchestra, Eugene Ormandy conducting. By the terms of an undisclosed agreement, the Lester piano had replaced Steinway as the official piano of the Philadelphia Orchestra, effective January 1, 1950. The Lester Piano Company, a Philadelphia-based organization, provided a specially constructed nine foot concert grand for use by the orchestra. Under the agreement, it was to be used as an instrument of the orchestra when a piano part was indicated in orchestral scores, but the Lester Company also seemed quite eager for this concert instrument to be used as a personal choice by a soloist. Since I was the orchestra's first piano soloist in 1950, I became the target of a highly concerted effort to influence me to make that choice. I was truly in a quandary. I wanted to use the Steinway because that was the piano I preferred, yet I did not want to "make any waves" with the Philadelphia Orchestra administration.

Then the light finally appeared to me. Since I was waiting for a confirmation of my invitation from the Steinway Company to become a Steinway Artist, I decided to attempt to accelerate the process. I rushed over to the Stetson Piano Company (the Philadelphia Steinway dealer) and pleaded, "Do it now!" so that I could tell "them" I am not allowed, under one agreement, to perform on another make of piano. They kindly consented and I was able to relate this reassuring information (reassuring to me, at least) to the Philadelphia Orchestra and to the Lester Piano Company. Reinforcing my end of the agreement, I procured a rubber stamp containing the inscription "Mr. Rezits plays the Steinway Piano"—and this message was carefully inserted on all the printed programs underneath the legend "The Lester Grand is the official piano of the Philadelphia Orchestra." Despite this elaborate plan, on the evening of the performance, the Lester Grand was positioned backstage next to the Steinway in case I might change my mind at the last minute. My father remained backstage near the two pianos, just to make sure that no mistake was made.

A scant two weeks after my appearance with the Philadelphia Orchestra, I was scheduled to perform the same Saint-Saëns concerto with the Terre Haute Symphony Orchestra. This fine orchestra was composed of members of the community as well as from the State Teachers College, now known as Indiana State University. It was an unseasonably warm day in late January and the community was adjusting in the expected way by opening windows, turning off the heat and so on. Although my memory is a bit vague about the building in which the concert hall was situated, I well remember that down somewhere in the subterranean regions there was a swimming pool. Since the heat of the day produced less than ideal temperature and humidity conditions in the pool area, the moist air was allowed to escape—providing an opportunity for droplets to find their way into the concert hall.

As we arrived at the hall for the afternoon rehearsal and opened the doors, clouds of moist air greeted us. Of course I immediately walked over to the piano to see how it was affected by this surprising development. Dear reader, have you ever seen a wet piano? One that is dripping (crying?) on the inside as well as the outside? Well, that's the way it was, and of course the order of the day was to clean it up. Some keys were already sticking on the way down, and when they arrived at the bottom of the key bed, they were reluctant to come up. Some high-power fans were brought in and I trust that every other means that could possibly be harnessed was brought into play. I cannot recall whether or not a rehearsal took place at that time. But I well remember that—miracle of miracles—by concert time that evening the piano was dry, worked perfectly, and the concert went on as scheduled.

I cannot conclude this narration without recounting my favorite but albeit brief "adventure" story from my colleague Menahem Pressler:

> "We [The Beaux Arts Trio] had rehearsed, and I found that one key was broken. I called the person in charge, and she said, 'Oh, we have a wonderful tuner, and you

mustn't worry about it. It will be all right. Well, we didn't worry. We came in the evening to the hall, and on the piano I found a little note. It said, 'Yes, I found out that key was broken. I couldn't do anything with it. DON'T USE THAT NOTE TOO MUCH!'"

⁎

The Day Grandma Ran Away

An excerpt from
A Kansas Sketchbook
By Elaine Lethem

My younger brother Bob and I were lucky to have a special grandma come live with us. It was better than having two mothers, for she seldom tried to discipline us. We were her only grandchildren. She focused all her love and attention on us.

She was a warm, cuddly grandma with a big soft lap. She liked our friends, and they liked her. She made our favorite foods—pancakes, custard pie, sugar cookies, biscuits. Grandma had no recipes. She used a handful of this and a pinch of that. When Mother or Dad punished one of us, we knew that Grandma sympathized. We would have been spoiled children except our mother would not allow it.

Mother worked well with her mother. They were used to it from Mother's growing-up days on the farm. They put out big washes once a week. When the clotheslines were full, they spread towels and aprons on the back hedge. They cleaned. They gardened. They canned. They made soap. They dressed chickens for the frozen food locker. Grandma did most of the ironing. Mother did most of the cooking. Grandma washed the dishes. She said she liked to wash dishes. They were congenial co-workers, and usually, ours was a peaceful, smoothly-running household. My dad always treated Grandma with kindness and respect.

Grandmother had been a Baptist, but she joined our Methodist Church when she came to live with us. However, she never lost some of the ideas from her early Baptist training.

Mother and Dad were products of their times—World War I, Women's Suffrage, the Roaring Twenties. Although their moral values were firmly rooted, they had relaxed considerably from the strict upbringing they knew as children. They had many friends and a busy social life. They were active in the community. Mother and Dad were up-to-date.

Mother tried to bring Grandma along to a more contemporary approach to life, and for the most part she succeeded. Grandma's clothes became more stylish. She liked to go to the picture show. She read current magazines. She enjoyed the radio. In many ways she became a modern woman. There were several areas, however, where Grandma's ideas could not be changed—ideas regarding women smoking, anyone drinking and everyone keeping their bodies decently clothed.

The last day of school, when I was eleven, became a day I have never forgotten. Some of my friends were wearing shorts. I wanted to be in style, and mother bought a pair of pink shorts for me to wear to the school picnic. When I came out for breakfast in my new outfit, Grandma's eyebrows shot up nearly to the knot of hair she wore on top of her head. A stern look of disapproval settled on her face. She said not a word, but we all knew that Grandma was upset.

Finally Grandma broke her silence, "Surely you are not going to let her go out of the house looking like that!" Mother went on calmly eating breakfast as she explained that lots of little girls were wearing shorts for playing. Grandma's answer was that no matter how many wore shorts, it was indecent for girls to show their legs.

When she realized that my mother's mind could not be changed, she stomped into her bedroom and slammed the door. A few minutes later she sailed through the house with her best hat jammed on her head and with a suitcase in her hand. Out the front door and down the street she marched.

I was alarmed. My mild-mannered grandmother had never behaved like this before. I think Mother was surprised too, but she sent Bob and me off to the picnic with our bowls of potato salad, and I soon forgot about the earlier crisis.

When the picnic was over and we'd gotten our final report cards, we started up the hill toward home. Then it all came rushing back. I wondered where Grandma was. We did not find her there when we got home, but Mother did not seem disturbed. She told us not to worry. A friend had called to say she'd seen our grandmother go into Mrs. Julian's house on South Poplar. It was impossible to walk down the street in our small Kansas town without at least a dozen people knowing it. A suitcase in the hand of the sedate Clara Kersey Brock must have caused quite a stir.

It seemed strange to sit down for supper at our big round kitchen table without Grandma. I felt sad, and I thought it was my fault. I was a model of good behavior that evening. I helped Mother clear the table and wash the dishes. We talked about the picnic, but I was thinking about Grandma.

I did not go out to play in the neighborhood, but sat on the porch swing watching down the street until long after dark. Too soon it was bedtime. Now I was really worried, but as I undressed in my room, I heard Grandma come in. For some reason, I did not go out to greet her. I think I felt embarrassed. Mother called to her, "Hello, I'm glad you're back." Grandma answered that she was very tired and needed to go to her room.

What a relief! Grandma had come home!

Next morning, nothing was said. To this day I do not know if Mother and Grandmother ever discussed it.

Now I'm a grandma, and as I see some of my dearly held values rejected, I feel a true empathy with Grandma Brock. I understand why she ran away from home.

✳

Performing in *Symphony of Six Million*

By June Miller

My performing art began very early in my life. I was three years old when all the children in the Indianapolis Mothers Jewels Methodist Church Sunday School put on a show for their parents. I was given a poem which my Mother taught me to say. There was no stage fright at that age. I remember that I just stood up by myself and recited the following:

"Wish I was a little rock sitting on a hill and doing nothing all the day but just sitting still. I wouldn't eat, I wouldn't sleep, I wouldn't even wash. I'd just sit there a thousand years and rest myself, oh by gosh!"

Everyone clapped and laughed and later patted me on the head and told me I had a spark, whatever that was. At any rate, a major step had been taken at age three, one that I would attempt to make again many times.

It was 1928 and my father and mother decided to "go west" and seek their fortune. As an only child, I had little to say, and at age eight I was enrolled in the Meglin School of Dance in Los Angeles. This is how my career in dancing, singing and performing began.

One day Mr. Meglin asked my mother to take me to RKO Pictures to try out for a role in a movie. I thought my mother would explode; her little precious person was going to be a movie star—she thought. We arrived at the studio and were taken to a set where there were many things going on: lots of loud shouting and lights galore. I was asked to stand up on a stage set so that everyone could see me. It was somewhat embarrassing, but overall it was exciting to be the center of attention.

One person ruffled my hair; another one took a special glass and looked at my eyes and face. Then someone else asked me my name and asked me to walk around so that they could see me in the lights. I was asked to play the piano, and then I knew I was not going to pass whatever test this was. In the midst of all this confusion, a very large man took me by the hand and said, "She looks like Birdie. She's just right for the part: even her dark eyes and hair. She is Birdie!"

And so my parents and I were asked to come to the RKO Studio the next day to settle a lot of business. What excitement in my house that night! And so I was launched into pictures with the help of Mr. Gregory Ratoff. I was to be his daughter in his American debut: the movie was titled "Symphony of Six Million," a Jewish saga, which turned out to be a true revelation of how a family grew up in the ghetto and succeeded. The other actors were Ricardo Corteg and Irene Dunne. My part was very small but it opened many doors for performing. During one dinner scene I was asked to eat gefilte fish and cold mashed potatoes. As soon as the cameras stopped, I quickly spat out all the food.

After the premiere showing at the Pantages Theater, a service was held at the Jewish Temple on Wilshire Boulevard. The Rabbi introduced everybody and mentioned that I was the only gentile in the film. I was so proud, and remained Ratoff's friend until he died. I was always his "Birdie."

Many years later, the Hebrew Department at Indiana University informed me that the film was to be seen on American Movie Classics.

She Always Played The Rose

By Nancy Seward Taylor

She always played the rose in their high school review. At the age of seven or so she would visit her father's bakery shop and eat her favorite green apple pie. Then she would skip over to what was then called the colored Baptist Church. Parishioners would help her into a pew where she dangled her legs and clapped her hands to their singing hymns. She loved their easy, happy rhythm.

She heard her father often speak of William Jennings Bryan and how powerful he was. Carrying an umbrella on a windy day she was carried up into the air. She yelled, "Billy Bryan, I'm being blown away!" One day she turned on the kitchen sink faucets but could not turn them off. "Help! Help! Billy Bryan, the water's running away!"

She was a member of one of the oldest families in Bloomington, and married into another one. When she was in her sophomore year at Indiana University, she went to the campus Well House where she met her beau. As is tradition he pinned his Phi Delta Theta pin under her Kappa Kappa Gamma key. That same year she had to move to Florida to take care of her mother, who had broken her hip. It had not set well. She wrote to her fiancé, "Now describe to me the new dance steps. I'm afraid when I return there will be a number of them I will have to learn."

When grown up she was described as one of the loveliest young women in Bloomington. She was Edith Eudora Regester Seward, my mother.

Power Tools

By Miriam Rosenzweig

My grandmother, born in 1869, grew up imbued with mid-Victorian mores and manners. My mother, who came along 21 years later, often complained of the slings and arrows inherent in her late-Victorian upbringing. I, in turn, was subjected to the remnants of that culture, although somewhat moderated by modernity. Mine was a post-Victorian childhood, filled with rules of decorum, and certain, swift punishment followed all infractions.

During my childhood, hugging, kissing and even touching was considered in bad taste—just not done. Members of my immediate and extended families expressed their approval or affection verbally, never by contact. And even that was meted out sparing. For better or worse, I probably transmitted much of that ethos to my own children, who were born in the decade of the '50s.

Then came the '60s. Manners and rules of behavior were swept aside, and everything was up for grabs. The young people told us that all human ills were the results of our inhibitions and reluctance to touch and feel our fellow creatures. Flower children taught us lessons about hugging and kissing along with permissive sex, tuning out and turning on. Most "over thirties" passed up sex and drugs, but we embraced the embrace. I was amazed by all the hugs and kisses I received from people I hardly knew.

I tend to think that such bodily gestures have little effect upon the human psyche and that humanity is not improved by the pecks we plant upon each other's cheeks. But hugging and kissing have become part of us, and, until recently, we practiced these contact sports with admirable skill. During the past few decades, however, the use and meaning of the touch have undergone a transformation, which some of us absorbed instinctively, while others had to learn it painfully. I learned my lesson through two distressing incidents.

A friend and I were invited to a party at the home of a senior university official. My friend had recently been to a good meeting with the host and felt warmly toward him. In that spirit, she entered his home, giving him a friendly hug. His response was to stiffen into a pillar of ice, leaving my friend confused and embarrassed.

Not having learned from her experience, I had to go through my own, a while later. Filled with admiration for a minister who had performed an interfaith family wedding with skill and grace, I threw my grateful arms around his shoulders. His body turned rigid with rejection, and I was humiliated.

My friend and I had obviously failed to notice the transformation of the cheek peck and hug from signs of affection to barometers of social standing. Appropriated by those who consider themselves superior, these formerly friendly gestures are now awarded to recipients of their choice. And woe unto those who don't know their positions on the social ladder. Unmistakable chill-out is their punishment. This is not to say that two friends hugging when they meet are not expressing sincere pleasure. The unspoken, but stern, rules apply on a more formal level of social intercourse.

It's a shame that the legacy of the flower children, intended to bring us closer together, has been turned into power tools, used to stratify society. But each generation creates the manners and mores reflective of its values. What do our reveal about us? ⁂

The Huckster

By Nevin W. Raber

When I was about fourteen, I had a high school buddy named Billy Smith. His uncle, Joe Smith, owned the village general store in Santa Fe, Miami County, in Indiana. Among the hundreds of items for sale at his store were canned fruit and vegetables, bread, crackers and cookies from large boxes with glass lids, pickles from a barrel, tobacco products of all types, denim overalls, gasoline and coal-oil.

The store's pine board floor had a deep, dark brown patina acquired from regular applications of oil, and the floor was swept daily. Near the middle of the store was a big, pot-bellied stove which heated the entire store during the cold winters. Around the stove were several chairs that had seen better days, and a nail keg surmounted by a hand-drawn checker-board. Almost daily, especially in cold weather, a few old-timers from the nearby farms and the village gathered to play checkers, swap tales, chew tobacco and spit in a box filled with sawdust.

Eldon, Joe's 35-year-old son, was the huckster. Joe owned an old ton and a half truck with a large box bed. Below a door in the back, some swing-down steps were attached that could be slid under the bed when not in use. Inside, along each side wall, were shelves with slats nailed to the front edge. These were designed to keep the contents from sliding off while the truck bounced along over the gravel roads. Slatted chicken crates were attached on each side under the truck bed. A swinging arm for hanging a spring scale was attached to the back near the door. The truck

as black; the box bed was painted green with SMITH GROCERY painted white in an arc on both sides.

On the morning when Eldon was scheduled to run his weekly route, he would stock the truck with items which were most desired by the farm wives. Most of these were staples not produced on the farm. Among them were canned fruits and vegetables; pins, needles and threads; flour, sugar, coffee; baloney rings, bacon slabs; fly-swatters; brooms and often a bolt of blue gingham with small white flowers. The total contents often exceeded a hundred different items.

Eldon would gas up the old truck and drive about a mile to my home which was in the living quarters of the near-by railroad station. Eldon always needed help, and we had agreed that I would work for my lunch. I would climb into the cab and we would start down Route 21 to begin our long day. I don't think Eldon had a set route, but he knew where his customers lived and just headed for the nearest one.

Eldon stopped near the front gate and honked the horn. The family dog began to bark, and the farm wife, who was waiting for us, came out carrying a basket with three dozen large, brown eggs to trade for her purchases.

Eldon would gas up the old truck and drive about a mile to my home which was in the living quarters of the near-by railroad station. Eldon always needed help, and we had agreed that I would work for my lunch. I would climb into the cab and we would start down Route 21 to begin our long day. I don't think Eldon had a set route, but he knew where his customers lived and just headed for the nearest one.

Eldon stopped near the front gate and honked the horn. The family dog began to bark, and the farm wife, who was waiting for us, came out carrying a basket with three dozen large eggs to trade for purchases. Eldon always had empty 24 dozen egg crates in the truck. I would take the basket and put the eggs in the crate. Then I would return the basket, write a sales check and enter the amount of credit due based on the market value of the eggs. The cost of the wife's purchases, which I wrote on the check, usually did not exceed the amount of credit, and I would return a little change. This was the middle of the Great Depression, and money was very scarce in this area.

We had a favorite spot for lunch which we always managed to reach about noon. This was in a customer's yard whose house stood on a small hill and was surrounded by great old oak trees which produced deep shade. About half way down the hill was a spring house. This small structure was built over a fast flowing spring which was encircled by a brick liner about five feet in diameter. This spring house was where the family kept their butter, milk and other perishables, for the water was cool and had a good flow the year around. The spring water was carried up to the house in buckets and was used for drinking, bathing and washing. The overflow went into a nearby tank for animals. Eldon and I would take our lunch—usually cheddar cheese and crackers—down to the spring house and eat in shade of those mighty oaks. We used the family's tin dipper to get a cool drink of water to wash down the cheese and crackers.

After lunch we continued on our route. The next farm wife we met carried out three plump Rhode Island Red hens which she had caught and penned up earlier in the day. She handed them to Eldon, and I hung the scales on the hook arm near the back door. Eldon strapped a hen's legs together and hung her on the scales. I wrote down the weight for each hen, totaled it, multiplied by the daily purchase price and wrote the credited amount on the sales check. The lady bought some thread; I totaled her bill and gave her the change. Eldon took each hen and stuffed her in one of the crates attached to the bottom of the truck bed.

It had been a good day. The egg crate and the chicken crates were filled and our inventory was depleted. Eldon headed the old truck back toward the station and dropped me off. He then drove back to the store, unloaded his eggs and chickens, removed any perishables from his cargo and parked the old truck until next week.

The huckster had run his route.

Christmas 2008

By Sue Gingles

Editor's note: Sue's husband Carl died in March '08. Following is her Christmas letter of that year.

Christmas is full of memories. Today I am remembering Kilimannbogo, an hour's drive from Nairobi, Kenya, where Carl and I spent the month of April 1995. Carl was volunteer dentist with the Rotary Club, and the dental clinic consisted of one room in a 60-bed hospital, run by Nigerian nuns. Carl spent Mondays and Fridays at the clinic and traveled to other places during the rest of the week. I was his cook, cleaner, laundress and companion. I became an admirer of the giraffes we saw loping gracefully along the fields beyond our quarters.

The village children played in the lane next to our house, and I often played games with them. One day, I drew a giraffe's head for them.

Every other week, the dentist visited a hospital-convent at Karieta, dedicated to the Immaculate Heart of Mary. On the drive there, we could view The Rift, and luscious, beautiful area. The trip involved an overnight stay at the convent, and I came along on the first trip. We slept on small beds in separate rooms. The nuns were gracious, and the food was delicious. After leaving Kilimannbogo, we went on a week's safari with Joseph, our guide. Here again, were lots of giraffes as well as other animals. This time, I was able to get close to them, which was a pleasure.

I am thankful for these memories and the fact that Carl was an adventurous type; and he seemed glad to have me tag along.

May you and your family have a blessed Christmas time. ⁑

Adventure in Fatehpur Sikri

By Jean Hermann

Fifty-nine years ago my husband and I, along with George age five, and Bill age three, were bouncing along a dusty, bad road in Pakistan to visit Fatehpur Sikri, a fabled city built in 1570 by the Mughal Emperor, Akbar. Our family followed my husband to many foreign ports and remote places for his work, and luckily, his parents were missionaries and he was accustomed to some of the strange sights, sounds, and smells we encountered.

On this trip, bouncing and bumping away on a rocky road, we saw an uncommon sight—trees. But no human beings were in evidence. Where was everybody? Suddenly we heard a loud thud on the roof of our car. This brought cries of fear from our boys, and my husband shouted, "Don't open the windows!" The loud thud was followed by the appearance of the black and white hairy face of a huge white gibbon hanging upside down outside our window. Soon, we felt some little thuds and tiny black-faced monkeys joined the grinning monster. A loud protracted blast from our car's horn surprised them, and we took the opportunity to speed away.

Looming just ahead of us was a large fortress that looked much like Jerusalem. Its height was impressive. Two geysers cascaded from the incredible height of the wall into a small pool below. A black speck in the stream became a young boy diver who had aced the hole and climbed out just before another diver arrived. Some tourists were throwing coins into the water to encourage the divers.

An old man, apparently the guide to the city, led us into the limestone fortress where we entered into near darkness and proceeded to march upward through narrow stairways and over occasional bridges which spanned unknown depth. All of the stone work was neat. Caves were hollowed out and, in some cases, decorated with low relief floral designs. Access to these spaces was knee-high above the floor because they were probably meant for merchants' displays. The merchants and their families probably slept there too but nowhere did we see much living space for many occupants.

My husband spoke Hindustani very well and the old guide was delighted. He agreed to show us the king's bedroom, not usually open to the public. It was built over a stream of water. Children collected flowers, bruised them, and tossed them by the basketful into the conduit where a perforated covering resembling lattice work allowed the aroma of the flowers to penetrate the cave and mask the odor of mold.

When we arrived at the upper level of the great wall, there was a vast expanse, filled with twelve majestic sandstone buildings in the Indian style of architecture. If there had been logos in those days, the symbol of Fatehpur Sikri would surely have been the *Anup Talao*, or *Open Court*, which dealt with serious crimes. The structure was a tank with a platform around it and four bridges leading up to it. Four jurors—one for every section of the city—determined the fate of the prisoner, shackled and lying at the bottom of the tank. Each juror ascended by his own stairway to a platform surrounding the ominous round tank where he could lean on a waist-high ledge surrounding the tank below to see the prisoner.

If declared innocent, the prisoner was free to go wherever he wished or to remain with his family. If declared guilty, his captors would lead him from the chamber, cross a bridge to a nearby hill, where the executioner waited. A huge tree trunk would have been pared to lie flat on the ground and an old gray elephant was shackled beside the worn path surrounding the headrest. The prisoner was spread-eagled, his hands and feet were attached to pegs in the ground. The elephant was then led around the condemned man several times for warm-up exercise and finally step on the man's head with his unshackled foot. So was justice administered.

We collected our family, paid the old guide, and continued our odyssey still wondering why there weren't more people here in such a great city. Further research revealed that, built on the banks of a lake that dried up, there was not sufficient water to support a community of 29,000 people. It was a ghost town by 1585—a magnificent but short life of 14 years.

Next stop: Agra and the Taj Mahal. ✲

The Pistol

By Richard P. Letsinger

My partner and I owned a real estate firm in Bloomington, Indiana. In addition to selling homes and commercial properties, farms, etc., we built some apartment complexes which were sorely needed in Bloomington. The Yorktown Court apartments were especially nice ones featuring town houses and a recreational facility and pool.

Our office employed a very competent rental administrator who managed and rented the apartments. I hardly ever knew who was living in this complex as I was very busy with other business matters. My partner was more involved with rentals than I was. He was a handsome Irishman who attracted the attention of many women, from all indications.

One day, I was very busy at my desk in my office when the secretary at the front desk called me on the intercom phone and announced a man wanted to speak to me. He and his wife rented an apartment at Yorktown Court. I had never noticed them except when they were in the office to rent their apartment. I thought he had a very homely wife. The man was the type who made practically no impression on a person other than being pleasant.

I stood up from my desk chair when the man came into my office and closed the door s he seemed to want privacy for discussing some personal business. When I turned around and seated myself, he sat down and placed a 45-caliber pistol in front of him on my desk,

with one hand on it. I shuddered a little, but had no idea why he did that, so I asked him what that was about.

With a perfectly even voice, the man told me he wanted to kill someone in the firm and since my partner was not in his office, I would do! Needless to say, this alarmed me a great deal and I began to think of how to escape from this situation before I was found lying dead across my desk.

With a strained voice, maybe even a trembling one, I asked why he was doing something like this and ruining the rest of his life . . . and mine too. He began to talk to me calmly and told his tale of woe. He claimed my partner had been making unwanted advances towards his wife. I could hardly think for a moment. While my partner was an attractive person and had inclinations to flirt with some women, I knew he would never have selected this man's wife for any attention. I had seen her, and she was far from beautiful.

I carefully chose my words and told this potential murderer that my partner never had any desire to compromise his wife in any way, and that this thought should not be in his mind whatsoever. I even began to think I was a psychologist and continued to talk pleasantly and with conviction—I thought. To my complete amazement, the man began to calm down, and he became talkative and began telling me of troubles with his wife and her illusions. I even began to think I needed to turn my shirt collar around backwards like a good priest's.

Immediately across the street from our downtown office, was the city police department. How I longed for an officer to appear and rescue me from behind my desk.

Barbara Restle

Then I began to think, and suddenly it came to mind that one of the policemen on duty was a man I had known for some time who was also a friend. I carefully picked up the telephone and called the front desk to my secretary who also knew this policeman. I asked my secretary if Boyd (the policeman's name) could come over and stop in my office to see me. My secretary was a very smart lady and recognized that something must be wrong in my office. She replied in an even tone that she would do it.

The man with the pistol in front of me asked what I was doing on the telephone, and I replied I had asked my secretary to call a man for me to cancel an appointment. He relaxed and sat back, but with his hand on the 45-caliber pistol. I was not home clear yet, and I sat with my elbows on the desk talking and chatting and hardly hearing what the man in front of me was saying.

Suddenly and quietly my office door opened and there stood my policeman friend with both arms in front of him and holding a gun pointed at the man in front of me. The policeman demanded the man take his hand off his gun and to put his arms up! I was in a complete state of terror but later the policeman said I looked calm. The man immediately did as the policeman told him and then they walked calmly out of my office and went across the street to the city jail.

My dear secretary got a raise that day! She came in my office to see how I had fared and found me just sitting there glaring at the wall where the man had sat in front of me. I soon pulled myself together and began thinking I had been in a dream. My secretary made me a cup of coffee and sat and chatted a few minutes and left me to thank my Maker for saving my life—for me a miracle.

The story did not end there. About three years later, I had a visitor in the office again. There stood the same man who was sent to the LaRur Carter Memorial Hospital, a mental rehabilitation center in Indianapolis.

I froze in my chair! NOT AGAIN, I thought.

This time, the man immediately shook my hand and sat down and began thanking me for saving his life and his family. He began to recite some of his previous difficulties and told me how happy he was that I had gotten him straightened out and well again. I was grateful for his recovery and mind, too! We parted friends, but I have never seen him again.

Crossword:

A Book Review
By Jane Layman

Crossword: One Man's Journey into American Crossword Obsession
By Marc Romano
Broadway Books 2005

Knowing my addiction to crossword puzzles, someone sent me this book from the Meadowood Library. I found it so intriguing that I felt obligated to tell others about it, even those who are not puzzle aficionados.

To begin with, the author states with no disclaimers that the compulsion to solve crossword puzzles is an addiction as persistent and powerful as addiction to alcohol or drugs. That in itself is such an extreme statement one thinks, "Hey, wait a minute . . . ." But using his own addiction experience as an example, he defends his statement with convincing data on the revenues realized by newspapers publishing a daily puzzle. Publishers of books of puzzles find those titles extremely profitable as well. Crossword puzzle solving has been called the most popular word game in history and an absolute windfall for publishers in every nation in the world.

The book describes the history of crosswords in the United States from 1913 to the present. The author devotes many sections to the evolution of today's puzzles—not only in difficulty, but in their relevance to an expression of popular culture. *The New York Times* can claim credit for making the daily puzzle a national pastime starting with a succession of editors from Margaret Farrar

to Eugene T. Maleska to Indiana University's own alumnus, Will Shortz who designed and completed his degree in Enigmatology before going on to law school. He assumed the helm of *The New York Times* puzzles in 1978, and things have never been the same. Shortz introduced a policy of escalating puzzle difficulty with Monday and Tuesday puzzles easier than those later in the week. The reader learns that construction of puzzles is a skill recognized and acclaimed, but Shortz is said to contribute about 50% of the clues. His standards are very high and he makes no compromises.

A section of the book covers the still mind-boggling story of how the *London Times* puzzle a few days before D-Day contained, as answers to clues, five code words for the invasion. Military intelligence people went berserk trying to find out if this was code to German spies or an unbelievable coincidence. To date, nothing has ever been unearthed but the (still unbelievable) conclusion that it was a coincidence.

With Shortz' leadership, an annual American Crossword Tournament has been held in Stamford, Connecticut, for about 30 years. The tournament attracts crossword experts from all over the world. The prizes are small; it is a chance for obscure people, often eccentric, who just happen to be good at this skill, to shine.

Romano covers the very basic difference between American and British puzzles. The British versions are described as cryptic; the clues are based on "inside" (national) jokes and usages, phrases and wordplay such as puns American clues are more factual with many sports and popular music references as well as motion picture lore. (We all know to whom Asta, the movie dog, belonged.) Romano claims that most American puzzle solvers, even expert ones, cannot do the British puzzles, while the average Brit can sit down and solve them with ease. Conversely they find our puzzles challenging, to say the least.

Solving crossword puzzles is recommended as a way for seniors to keep brain cells stimulated, so the time spent on a favorite pastime can be comfortably justified.

This small volume is fun to read even if readers are not puzzle solvers; but if they are cruciverbalists, they will find themselves in a six-letter word for paradise. ⁂

Ed. note: Asta the movie dog, a wire-haired fox terrier, starred in *The Thin Man* movies among others . . . and appears in many crossword puzzles, too.

Bees Do it. Birds Do it. Blue-footed Boobies And Whales Do It

By Barbara Restle

I have always wished to see whales up close. To do this I joined fifteen serous nature lovers from Europe and boarded a ninety-foot ship in San Diego, a ship with cabins the size of our Meadowood bathrooms. A galley for socializing and meals provided benches and tables nailed to the floor. Our seven cheerful sea-hardened crew members and Captain Art made every effort to keep us safe and as comfortable as was possible in what was termed the "rolling seas" of the Pacific: seas that rolled our ship into thirty-five degree lists. After boarding, I was led down a steep narrow staircase to my cabin, by a welcoming and broadly smiling crew member. His tanned face deeply lined after many years at sea, he introduced himself as Lambchop, the dishwasher. On this ship, crewed by seven American men and Captain Art, every man had multiple jobs.

Lambchop opened my cabin door and, with a muffled grunt, lifted my large suitcase to the upper bunk. In a low voice he said, "Brought your own cabin mate on board, I see." Before I could respond, he said, "Close quarters, but you'll only be in your cabin to sleep", and he left. With my cabin door closed, there was only enough space to duck my head and slide into my bunk. I could not sit on my bunk. I did have a private miniature sink with a cold water tap with two small shelves overhead.

For two weeks, fifteen nature enthusiasts gratefully, without the comforts of the 21st century, lived out their dreams, to visit the animals only seen on TV nature programs. We had also been requested not to bring any electronic devices for communicating with the outside world. We were encouraged to go back in time and to experience a world not touched by modern technology.

During daylight hours, we had a crew member who climbed up to the crow's nest to spot the blowing, spouting whales. Often the whales were in a pod swimming toward feeding areas.

When we sailed around San Benito Island, we were about halfway between San Diego and Cabo San Lucas (a city that Meadowood residents visited in 2008). San Benito Island is well known as the calving area for whales and we were fortunate in seeing several finback whales and their calves. The finback whales are the second largest whales and feed primarily on small fish.

The most memorable sighting was the largest of all whales, a blue whale with her new-born calf, which appeared to intentionally bring her calf alongside our ship for a fifteen minute visit. I was leaning over the deck rail when she spouted out of her huge blow holes and I felt the mist on my face. Somehow, as ridiculous as this sounds, I felt blessed. This modern whale's ancestor lived in our oceans more than fifty million years ago. This blue whale was longer than our ninety-foot ship and the calf, only a few weeks old, was between twenty-three and twenty-five feet long. We were told that to see a blue whale and her calf this close was rare. On another day we also saw five blue whales in a pod without calves. The birthing of all whale calves is in February, and the ocean around the Baja Peninsula is where Pacific Ocean whales come for birthing. Within a few months, the mothers guide their calves to the Arctic regions, where the mothers are able to feed again.

Late one afternoon, our captain dropped anchor close to a pyramid-shaped mountain. On a stone ledge several hundred feet above the rolling sea, a pair of blue footed booby sea birds danced, their long pointed bills clicking together, their necks intertwined: all symptoms of love-bonding. Their blue-webbed feet, as large as our own hands, quick-stepped to an ancestral rhythm. The nesting site of this bonded pair was halfway up a mountainous rock in the Sea of Cortez that separates the mainland of Mexico from the Baja Peninsula. This craggy mountain jutting out of a blue-green sea had no vegetation to adorn it; hardly a scene for a romantic encounter. Hundreds of sea birds with loud ear-piercing laments challenged each other over nesting sites or perching areas.

A booby is a fish-eating bird, found in tropical and sub-tropical waters. Its nesting sites are barren rock, and how they keep their eggs from falling into the ocean is a marvel of Darwin's theory of natural selection. The chicken lays her eggs in a carefully planned round nest that protects an egg from rolling out. The eagles build their round twiggy nests hundreds of feet on top of a tree hundreds of years old. The booby, however, can only lay her egg on a tilted mountain ledge and due to its design, the booby egg only turns in circles with little chance it will role into the sea.

On this late afternoon, the mountain was surrounded by flying yellow-footed gulls, white and brown pelicans, frigate birds, various species of herons, albatrosses and egrets. There was a good reason this mountain was white: it was covered with guano. The next hurricane would likely scour its surface clean, if only temporarily, returning phosphates and nitrogen to the sea.

Do I recommend sailing for two weeks on the Pacific Ocean and Sea of Cortez in a small ship in a rolling sea? I hesitate to do so. There were too many times I needed to dash to my bunk when the captain announced, "Heading for rough seas!" Early in the trip, when I neglected to respond, the bruises to my face and various parts of my body turned an embarrassing purple. Would I do it again? Yes, of course, in my sixties but not in my _____. **

Help! Anyone? Help!

By Libby Buck

The day started out as just another day of multi-tasking. I shopped for groceries and carried my bags to my Toyota and placed them in the passenger seat. My next stop was a doctor's appointment. I parked the car in the Internal Medicine Associates (IMA) parking lot and after a consultation with my doctor, returned to my car and found it impossible to open the door on the driver's side. A large Cadillac had parked so close to my car, even a size six woman would have had to struggle to squeeze into my car.

I considered all options available to me and knew that returning to IMA and finding the owner of the Cadillac was not one to pursue. I took all the grocery bags out of the front seat and placed them in the back seat. I climbed into the passenger seat with some difficulty, slowly moved myself over the gear shift separating the driver's seat from the passenger seat. The move was not successful. I landed on my back in the driver's seat with one leg trapped under the gearshift. My head was wedged against the driver's side door and soon my neck began to cramp. I lay in this awkward position for several minutes, again considering my options. I decided that I must open the door to ease the pressure on my neck and found that I could open the door with my right hand, the left one wedged under my body. The door quickly swung open as far as it could and hit the door of the Cadillac. My head dropped out the door, leaving me in a far more awkward position than before. With my leg totally trapped under the gearshift, my head hanging out the door, one arm trapped under my body, I was now incapacitated. I only had one option left to me. I yelled: "Help! Will someone help me?"

Soon I heard the voice of a man ask, "Is there something I can do for you?" Under the circumstance I thought the question was not appropriate or necessary. He was an older man of small stature and I wasn't sure he was strong enough to do the job of extricating my leg from under the gear shift. However, I answered him, "Please try to free my leg. Then I think I can manage to sit up."

He said, "Give me the keys so I can turn on the engine and so I can change gears and then you can get your leg loose."

The keys were in the pocket I was lying on. There was no way anyone could reach them. When the man learned of this, the only option was to call out "Help'" several times as loud

Barbara Restle

as he could in all directions of the IMA parking lot. Soon another older man, with a more robust build, appeared and told the first helper to lift and hold up my head while he pushed and then lifted my leg from under the gear shift.

Gratefully, I could now sit up. I said, "Thank you very much. The two of you working together helped me out of a truly awkward position. Again I thank you."

I got the keys out of my pocket and started the engine, ready to leave, when I heard the second man call out, "Wait for your husband. He isn't in the car yet." The first helper announced with an affirmative tone. "This woman is not my wife." I heard the second helper reply, "For the sake of our own safety, let's wait until she is out of the IMA parking lot." ⁂

A Letter to Barbara

By Bernard Clayton Jr.

Dear Barbara Walters—

I have read your book but what about us, Barbara, you and me?

Your memoir, *Audition*, listed as a bestselling book by *The New York Times*, treats us with presidents, prime ministers, kings and queens, nabobs and knaves, but you don't mention us.

Not once. Pity. I remember it well!

It was during the 1974 holidays. I had written *Bernard Clayton's The Complete Book of Breads*. NBC had invited me to come to New York with an assortment of breads and do a bread-making demonstration on the "Today Show."

I arrived at the NBC studio with the basket of loaves I had baked in Indiana, plus several baked earlier that morning in the kitchen of the Algonquin Hotel. I was loaded with loaves!

At the NBC studio I was ushered into a guest waiting room and met a fellow guest, John Lennon. We nodded and spoke briefly. I decided to tour the behind-the-camera facilities rather than just sit.

Barbara, we did not get off to a good start. I knew it by the tone of your voice over the P.A. system: "Where's the man from Indiana who's going to make bread? He's not here where he should be!"

On camera things were fine. We cut and nibbled about half dozen breads and then turned to making a loaf. You quickly got into the baking mode: you took off rings so you could get your hands into the dough.

Yes, I should have warned you about my spirited finale to show that you must knead the dough with vigor—forget tenderness!

I raised the four-pound ball of dough head-high and slammed it down on the table covered with a generous sprinkling of flour. The dough landed amidst an explosion of white flour. Flour covered us both.

There was a frantic whisper at my side, "Oh, no! This dress is borrowed!" When the broadcast was over, you gave the ultra suede dress a final brush, reached for a loaf to take home and left.

I gave the crew the leftover breads, shook the flour off my apron and returned to Indiana.

I remember it well.

Sincerely,
Bernard Clayton Jr. ⚜

Never Found Myself

*From a fictional story by
Frances H. Sanden 1908-2005*

Many young people today speak of "finding themselves." Like Diogenes with his lantern, they search the highways and byways hoping to capture that most elusive will-of-the-wisp happiness.

Recently, I was the uncomfortable witness to my young grandson taking leave of his home and parents to "find himself." For the occasion, he departed in a suede jacket, woodsman boots and a well-filled backpack, all from an expensive outfitter. He left his mother in tears and his father alternating between rage and concern, as well as bereft of a substantial amount of "borrowed bread".

I wished him well, told him to keep in touch and promised to guard the home fires during his absence. As I said goodbye, nostalgia swept over me and the past became the present. I found myself in my mother's kitchen, the favorite room for every member of our tightly-knit family.

Mama was making bread. She looked up expectantly as I entered the room and gave her a hug. She faced me. "You home so early?" She smiled happily. "I knew you'd find work right away. A fine looking young man like you who even played football in college."

"I don't want to find a job that fast," I began. I gulped and paused for courage. "Besides, I'm not sure I even WANT a job."

Mama looked at me in astonishment. "You don't want a job. A millionaire you should be."

"It isn't that, Mama. I just want to 'find myself' before I'm chained to a job for life."

Mama kneaded the bread with extraordinary vigor, pounding and slapping it was though it were a living thing in need of punishment. "You want to find yourself! When did you get lost? Go look in the mirror and pinch yourself. You'll notice you're here all right."

I found myself feeling hot and went to the refrigerator to pour a glass of milk, stalling for time. "You don't understand. I want to know what makes me 'tick.' I want to become a whole person."

Mama dusted the flour from her hands and laughed. "Whole, you want to be? Look, Sammy, the only hole you've got to worry about is the one in your head from all your crazy ideas."

I groaned aloud. Did anyone in all of history ever have such an unsympathetic parent?

"I don't know why I even bother to try to explain. You always twist everything around so I look ridiculous."

Mama settled into the old rocker where we were rocked to sleep when we were babies. I wished she wouldn't. It brought back memories, like the time I had the mumps and she sat up with me all one night even though she had to go to work early the next morning.

I started out slowly, as though talking to an illiterate. "Mama, I know it's hard for you to

Barbara Restle

accept, but I might as well get it over with. I'm going to put off finding a job until I

know what will make me happy."

Mama snickered and nodded approvingly. "How nice! How great!" Her mood suddenly did an-about face as she recalled past sacrifices. "I suppose your papa was singing all day and night when he worked overtime to put you through college. I know you think I danced to work every morning at 6:30 a.m. to do alterations."

My face reddened with shame and then I became defensive. I knew they worked hard. I got reminded of it often enough—only so did I. It's no fun to get knocked around a football field for practice, especially if you're never recognized as a big campus hero. "Things are different now, Mama. You're always talking about the Depression days. People live easier now."

Mama nodded her head in agreement. "Thank God for that," she said devoutly. She paused, then stared at me intently. It was the same look I received when I was ten years old and failed to live up to Mama's expectations. "How are you going to live so good if you don't have a job? Believe me, it's not better you'll live—it's worse. I know."

"I'll get along," I answered coolly, and reached for a cookie from the permanently filled cookie jar.

Mama always met a challenge head-on. "How?" she demanded.

I munched on a cookie and took a long drink of milk to give me stamina. "I'm going to

travel to America. I'll pick up jobs as I go along."

Mama took a new tack and hit the bull's eye. "What about Jenny?"

I tried to look unconcerned. "What about her?"

Mama shot the arrow straight through my heart. I responded by leaning back in my chair as far as its spindly back legs would carry me, as though trying to dodge the onslaught. "Jenny's not going to wait while you run around American strumming your ukulele and living like a bum."

I answered with more confidence than I felt. "If she loves me she will."

Mama laughed indulgently. "If she loves you! She can also love Hymie Katz. He has a good job and is already a bank teller—and no college either." She went back to check her bread and sent the final shot, "Easier for a girl to love someone with money than a bum with a busted ukulele."

I was completely frustrated and shouted, "Mama, I'm just not ready to get married yet. I refuse to be chained to a nine-to-five way of life."

My equally frustrated parent raised her hands and looked to the heavens as though for strength to continue the conversation with her idiot offspring. "Thousands of dollars we spend on your education and what do we get? A graduate who left behind his brains!

It was unfinished symphonies like this, plus the prospect of ditching a comfortable and inexpensive way of life that persuaded me to change my line of thought. Another powerful influence, due to the constant and persistent horror stories related by my parents, was the specter of another Depression strangling me in its grip.

So I went to work, got married, had children, lived an ordinary life with ordinary people, and never did learn if I had found myself. On the other side of the coin, however, is the comforting thought that I never was entirely sure I had lost myself—wholly, or in part. All I do know is that I've been happy . . . "doing what comes naturally."

I have no doubt my rebel grandson will, in his own way and time, do the same.

Cocktails Anyone?

By Ernest Campaigne

Do you ever wonder why we name tasty aperitifs after a rooster's tail feathers? There are all kinds of cocktails. In addition to the hundreds of alcoholic drinks, we have seafood cocktails, fruit cocktails and so on. The word "cocktail" is an American word that has its origins in New Orleans in the early 1800's.

Citizens of New Orleans in the early days were in the habit of taking a spoonful of bitters daily to prevent the "ague," a prevalent disease of that swampy area where people were prone to malaria. "Bitters" are concoctions of herbs and spices in alcohol or water used as stomachic's and in cooking as a flavoring. It was the habit of the gentry to stop at a bar on Bourbon Street for a spoonful of their favorite bitters. Since the bitters went down a little easier when mixed with brandy, the bartender looked for a small drinking vessel to serve the mixture of a spoonful of bitters and a spoonful or two of brandy. He decided egg cups were just the right size, and began serving his bitters mixtures in them. His porcelain egg cups, from England, each had a picture of a rooster with a luxuriant red tail.

So the citizens of New Orleans began requesting their daily dose of stomachic as "the cocktail." It was not long before this word had spread to the major cities. By 1860, a mixture of bitters, gin and vermouth was being served in San Francisco. It was called a "Martinez" cocktail, after the town and county north of the city where it supposedly originated. This drink migrated to New York and Boston and evolved into the present day martini. New York bartenders soon created their own cocktail, a "Manhattan," a mixture of rye whiskey, bitters and sweet vermouth. By the 1880's a number of new cocktails were listed in bartender's guides of the time.

Some menus show that cocktails were served in American bars in England and France in the early days of the twentieth century, but they didn't become common until after World War I. The American Expeditionary Force (A.E.F.) introduced cocktails generally to Europe, and brought back their own creation, a "French 75," named after French artillery, composed of champagne and brandy with or without bitters. Cocktails really took off during the Roaring Twenties, with bartenders everywhere in the United States creating their own variations. A recipe book lists 201 recipes for the martini alone (*The Martini Book* by Sally Ann Beck, Workman, NY, 1997.)

In recent years, liqueurs have largely replaced bitters as a flavoring agent, and a wide variety of garnishes have been added. For example, the Gibson, first served at the Gibson Hotel in Cincinnati, is simply a martini garnished with a pearl onion instead of an olive. The basic recipe for a cocktail, known as the "1, 2, 3 Cocktail" is: one part sour, two parts sweet and three parts strong. The "Bass Boot," popular in Maine, was created by a scion of the Bass Shoe Company and is one part lemon juice, two parts maple syrup and three parts rye whiskey.

So try your own hand at a 1, 2, 3 Cocktail. If it tastes good, you might become famous!

❖

Lost in Pronunciation

By Olympia Barbera

As told to Rosemary Messick

Shortly after we opened the door on arriving home from vacation, we discovered our home in a shambles. Just then the phone rang.

"Hello . . ."

"Olympia, how grand that you're back! I'm calling to remind you of our Guild meeting tomorrow. Shall I pick you up?"

"Oh Rowena, I can't go. We walked in on a terrible mess. The "keds" have peed under the piano! I'll have to spend tomorrow cleaning up the whole house."

"You left them alone?"

"Oh, yes. We always have."

"Do they know how to take care of themselves?"

"Sure. They always do. When I'm here they behave perfectly. I don't know what happened this time."

"How many kids do you have?"

"The first we adopted when we bought this house since he was already living here."

"Really? And the second?"

"My son brought the second one home from college. So we adopted it."

"Oh my! How old are they now?"

"Oh, I don't really know. I can't remember how long we've had them."

"I see. You say they usually behave themselves?"

"Oh, sure! They know what to do. All I have to do is feed them and be sure they have something to drink."

"Really? Do you think they may be sick? Maybe that's what caused them to lose control."

"I guess they might be. Looks like they may have vomited some."

"Don't you think you should have them seen by a doctor?"

"I don't know. I'm thinking about that. But, if I take them anyplace, it will be to a vet."

"A vet? What do you mean? How many kids did you say you have. I thought you had three."

"Wait a minute Rowena! What are we talking about here?"

"I didn't know you had two younger kids too."

"Oh, no! I have three children. They're all in college. It was the "keds" that made the mess."

"I still don't understand."

Barbara Restle

"My 'keds'—k-i-d-s, are grown. It's my 'keds',
c-a-t-s, I'm talking about."

"You mean cats?"

"Yes, I mean 'keds!'

Something was lost in pronunciation. ⚹

A Prayerful Moment

By Bill Baldwin

Baseball was an important sport in Northwest Conference schools. During my college days it drew sizable crowds of students and town folk during the first warm days of spring. Pete Jongs was Pacific University's baseball coach, chosen because he had pitched one season for the Boston Braves before entering military service.

Pete was a dogged student. He refused to let a study session end until he understood the assigned material. It must have been that same dogged determination that had made him a major league pitcher. At five feet six inches and a bit rotund, he lacked those physical attributes that characterize most successful hurlers. We studied together and Pete refused to leave a topic until he had it thoroughly in mind. His determination also served me well.

Pete's drive to succeed had much to do with the improved fortunes of our baseball team. We were leading the conference standings when we visited Whitman College on a balmy day in May. The athletic teams were named the Missionaries because of the school's strong religious affiliation. Pacific teams were Boxers for no discernible reason. But Peter's sparring instincts became well known around the conference. He had a well-deserved reputation for finding fault with umpires and verbally assaulting their decisions—a coaching tactic rarely practiced by his fellow coaches.

During an early inning, Coach Pete had seen enough. What he saw as an obvious ball, the ump called a strike. Pete stepped from the dugout, yelling protests as he approached the object of his disdain. Before he could begin his usual series of gesticulations, a gentleman wearing a clerical collar stationed himself in front of the assembled crowd and stood and under his obviously professorial direction sang a full verse of "Tell Your Troubles to Jesus." Pete was well versed in spotting humor in any situation. He stopped short, removed his cap, bowed his head, and stood in motionless attention until the choral leader directed the chorus to sit. And that's what Pete did.

Two innings later when the umpire sinned again, Pete strode to the third base box—halting play—removed his cap and knelt prayerfully while holding an eye chart. He had planned his own bit of high jinks *vis-á-vis* the umpires.

The Missionaries provided the loftiest possible setting!

*
**

Barbara Restle

A Good Yokefellow: Please

By Beth Van Vorst Gray

It's the story of oxen, you know. Oxen are destined to be a lifelong team that pulls a cart. In preparation for this, a pair is roped together almost from birth so the long horns of each grow in the direction away from their yoke mate. Raised in this manner, they do not poke into each other as they move the weight of their burden forward.

Upon hearing this revelatory news, I decided that it was *my* horns, though barely visible, that are getting in the way of developing a lasting, satisfying lifetime relationship. Although, biologically, I can't be an ox since I am female, I relate to the "horns" problem. I wasn't yoked early enough or perhaps it just didn't take and I have charted my own course for too many years. My horns weave this way and that splaying about in every direction as I search for my spiritual center, a vocation (I've had three separate and distinct ones), and some pleasures along the way. This has been altogether satisfactory until now, but, as my thoughts turn towards forming a lifelong commitment, I see that this has not prepared me very well for a yoking.

I was blessed with a good brain, body, and a work ethic that has given me the means to take care of my family and meet my own needs. There have been wonderful companions to share this journey with me and help me learn the lessons of life. My heart is telling me now that partnership is the way to go. In a good pairing, trouble is halved and joy is tripled. Since it is much too late in life to re-invent me, perhaps I should submit a personal ad, reading:

"Lady ox whose horns lean mostly to the right, who has carried life's baggage over treacherous trails in a cart drawn by one, is seeking a yokefellow whose horns are slightly left-leaning, has secure footing, and whose meter and stride are flexible—a bit of the blues, some lively jazz, and a little night music once in a while."

⁂

Reprinted with permission from *Kitchen Table Talk*, Gray Matters Press and IBJ Custom Printing, Indianapolis, 2009.

Lost in Translation

By Norman Overly

In Japan, space is at a premium. Houses and businesses are crowded together with minimal room for narrow roads and even narrower walk ways, snaking between houses and garden plots. (You can't call them sidewalks because pedestrians share them with all manner of vehicles.) However, even the humblest and smallest of homes is likely to have a focal point near the entrance that features a bit of isolated nature. Here one may meditate or at least be reminded that in the littlest space, a practiced eye may find stimuli for reflection. A four by four foot space is enough to have a small shrub and a carefully selected stone or lantern or other attractive bit of nature displayed and nurtured. Sliding open the shoji (white paper-covered door) lets a bit of nature into an otherwise plain small room. As I lived in Japan I became more and more interested in the use of space and dimple artifacts to suggest vast vistas and bring nature into contact with daily life.

We had been living in Japan for three years in a cliffside home in the center of Yokohama. I became aware that the five stamp-sized gardens around our house were being overrun by the invasive Kuzu (kudzu) and the ubiquitous take (bamboo) that massed as a solid green web between our home and the city some 60 feet below. Both plants served to secure the hillside upon which our home was perched like a hulking gray bird of prey watching the city below. I had no idea how the little triangular terraces had been groomed in the past, but I was aware that the kudzu was growing a foot a day and threatening to overwhelm everything in its way. The 5 X 15 foot triangular clothes line garden on the east side had vines and bamboo threatening the poles and lines. Something had to be done. I decided to put in a lawn.

I began hacking and tugging. With much effort, I cleared the lowest terrace of invading vines and was rewarded in a few weeks by a carpet of dandelions, plantain, clover and other heat resistant weeds. It was green and looked like the lawn I had grown up with in northern Ohio. Now I needed to find a way to maintain it. I searched the little shops in the neighborhood and ultimately found an old push mower with iron wheels and cutting mechanism as well as a rough wooden handle. I located a file and honed the blades. After months of labor I finally had my lawn, four small triangles of green weeds, neatly trimmed. (The laundry garden remained—packed dirt and a narrow cement walk.)

Alas, the kudzu and bamboo continued to grow up the hill and over the chain link fence that outlined the boundary of the property. I decided that help was needed to keep the vegetation at bay. The hillside growth had to be cut back, if not rooted out. I inquired for someone who could do the job. Upon locating a woman who was willing to do the work, I explained in my best Japanese that I wanted the hillside bamboo and kudzu cut back. I went on to explain that I was making a lawn (*shibafu*) that I wished to mow and that the wild grasses (kudzu and bamboo) were defeating me. The engaged worker nodded knowingly and agreed that the offending weeds would be gone. At least that was my understanding.

As chance would have it, a friend arrived from America to visit us for a few weeks. Because Jeanne was nursing our month-old son, I was enlisted to serve as the tour guide. Off we went to visit the western provinces and experience old Japanese cultural treasures. Ten days later, when I arrived back in Yokohama, my uncomprehending eyes were greeted by four gardens devoid of a single blade of grass, weeds or any other greenery. The soil was tamped down firmly and it had been swept clean.

I stormed into the house and asked Jeanne what had been going on. She said she assumed they were doing what I had asked them to do. I was crestfallen. I rushed outside where a trio of women was on their knees pulling up the last of the reluctant dandelions and plantain as they finished their work. I asked, "Why did you pull up all my *shibafu*? She responded, "*Sensei* (teacher) that is not *shibafu*; that is weeds!"

They had worked for nearly two weeks carefully undoing my labor of love. It was an expensive lesson. I checked my dictionary again. Sure enough, *shibafu* means lawn, as on the greens of a golf course! (In Japan you seldom see green grass except on a golf course.) Everything else is a garden with limited ornamental grass. My lawn was not to be. I had four well-kept, irregularly shaped dirt patches that awaited someone else to put in a stone lantern, a tiny *koi* pond and a miniature pine tree. When in Japan, do as the Japanese do. No *Shibafu*. ⁂

Hamlet and Cyrano de Bergerac

By Oswald Ragatz

I was very fortunate to experience classes with several fine teachers during my four years in high school. One of the most notable of these was Mrs. Jones. Mrs. E.T.C. Jones. I never knew what the initials stood for, but they did serve to separate this particular woman from the myriad Mrs. Joneses of the world.

Characteristics of my Mrs. Jones included imagination, enthusiasm, commitment, energy and personal warmth. Only her lack of judgment would prevent me from calling her a great teacher. She was our English teacher and coach for school plays.

The first semester of my junior year was spent rewriting Shakespeare's Hamlet in modern English blank verse, thus giving the students a unique in-depth understanding of the story and of the author's genre. The second semester we presented the drama in modern dress, a successful endeavor that greatly impressed the community. For the play, Mrs. Jones obtained from somewhere fluorescent material that in black light made an impressive costume for the ghost of Hamlet's father.

Goaded on by Hamlet's stellar success, Mrs. Jones chose for our senior play that late 19th century poet-dramatist Edmond Rostand's *Cyrano de Bergerac*. Back from a summer trip to New York, Mrs. Jones was excited by Broadway's use of projected scenery. This would be her next triumph. In Act 3 of our Cyrano, the garden scene was projected on the rear wall of the stage. Here, in the shadow of garden shrubbery, Roxanne is being wooed by Cyrano's friend because Cyrano is embarrassed by his unsightly large nose.

One problem Mrs. Jones hadn't thought of . . . this was no Broadway theater stage. The high school had been built in the first decade of the 20th century. (My mother had gone to school in this building!) There was about two feet between the cyclorama and the back wall. No problem. We'd just project the scene from the balcony. The small slide projector was not even state-of-the-art in 1935. No problem. The new light bulb made the projector so hot it was in danger of self-destructing. No problem, said the boy operating the projector. He'd just bring his bicycle tire pump and blow cooling air on the hot apparatus.

But there was a major problem with all this, and no solution. The action on the stage was between the projector and the rear wall, thus enormous shadows were seen in motion on the backdrop of garden scene. At that point, Mrs. Jones gave up. It would just have to do, shadows and all. But wait! More disasters. The projector was placed on a flimsy table, which jiggled with every plunge of the bicycle pump's handle. This motion was catastrophic to the scene on stage, and furthermore the pump squeaked with each plunge. These last features did not become apparent until the performance, however, so the pathos of Act 3 was presented with a background visual of a garden bouncing up and down about a foot or two, accompanied by rhythmic squeaks from the balcony. This, while the actors were emoting, by proxy, passionate love.

I don't remember any disasters in Act 4. I do remember a feeling of restlessness in the audience. But wait! There is Act 5. We had

Barbara Restle

borrowed a wheezy pump organ from the Catholic grade school. The act must take place in a church yard, since I was to play suitable "churchy" music during the final tragic scene. As usual, I had not been chosen to play the lead—wrong persona and most unsuitable voice. But I was usually the lead man's best friend. Cyrano's friend, however, proved to be rather feckless.

We had rigged up our own costumes, and I had a spectacular hat involving a black ostrich plume borrowed from an old hat of my mother's. It was by far the most impressive hat of the production. Well, Bill Corbridge (Cyrano) had somehow lost his hat during Act 4. By then, I think I probably was fed up with the whole show. As Bill was to make his entrance he asked me for my hat. I'm ashamed to say that I refused. He went on with his big act bareheaded, hating his faithful friend (me) until my final exit backstage to my noisy pump organ.

I wasn't onstage for the final disaster. Set in the churchyard was a large tree, with branches hanging eight feet from the floor, where they connected to the trunk. But the trunk had not been secured to the floor by the stage crew. Weeping Cyrano leans on the trunk which wobbles away from its top while Cyrano tries to right himself. The curtain falls, it is midnight, the audience wakens and departs midst laughter. There was no post-performance celebration. Mrs. E.T.C. Jones went into seclusion for several days and most of the "actors" went off to college and never darkened a stage again. ⚹

Nothing

By Henry H. Gray

For the past few days I have had nothing on my mind. That is to say, nothing has been puzzling me, and a lot of my thinking has led to nothing. It seems that nothing can be defined only by something. In other words, nothing is nothing in the absence of something, or perhaps anything, or everything. A few other words are like that. Darkness is the absence of light; silence is the absence of sound. There can be no nothing without something.

Without realizing it, human beings had nothing for a long time but still knew nothing about nothing. The Greeks didn't wander about asking each other "Do you know what nothing is?" The Romans had numbers but no nothing. After a lot of thought, the Muslims finally found nothing, but they called it zero. One cannot really do nothing. The small boy who said he went out and did nothing really isn't thinking about nothing. Nothing is like McAvity, it isn't there.

I've tried hard to think about nothing, but it's difficult because there is nothing there to think about. It's like trying to achieve absolute zero. You can't get there. And what will you do when you do get there? This brings up another thought. When I was ten or twelve, I was told, in answer to a question, "We're half way there." In a sudden epiphany (is there any other kind?) I realized that if we again got half way there, and again, and again, we would never get there! I have yet to put this gem of wisdom to any real use; I hope somebody can. But it's not nothing.

I read not long ago that the Ark of the Covenant is in safekeeping in Ethiopia. No one is allowed to see it. It is simply there; no use asking questions. So it might as well be nothing. I also read of an Eastern holy man who told a visiting engineer that the world rested on the back of a huge turtle. The engineer asked what that turtle stood on. *An even larger turtle*, was the reply. After a few more such questions the holy man put up his hand. "Stop!" he said. "I know what you're thinking, but it's no use. It is turtles all the way down!" In other words, it's turtles or nothing.

Nothing is not chaos; chaos is the absence of order in something. Astrophysicists are still looking into that one, but even they haven't found nothing. Atheism is another word that is defined only by contrast with something else. That is, atheists think that god is nothing. Perhaps that is the best proof that God exists.

As you see, I really have nothing on my mind. Sometimes I have nothing to say, but it seems I will always have nothing to think about.

**

Barbara Restle

Fighting for Iris

By Bernard Clayton Jr.

A gun in school is nothing new. It was 72 years ago when I was a high school senior, one in a class of 38 students. Jamie Beck brought a gun to school and told his friends he was going to shoot me. He showed them the gun. I was later told it was a shiny silver-plated 22 mm pistol.

It was all because of Iris, the cutest girl in the class, with bangs like Clara Bow, a neat figure and always immaculately dressed, (thanks to a doting mother.)

Every boy in school at one time or other had a crush on Iris. This time it was Jamie who took exception to my taking Iris to the movies. It was in the depths of the Great Depression and going to the theater with me was something special because I had passes to theaters in Indianapolis, thanks to their advertising in my Dad's newspaper. I also had my Dad's car and gas was a dime. Jamie thought that was an unfair advantage.

He did not shoot me that day, but one night a week later after I escorted Iris to her door, I walked back down the driveway to find Jamie waiting for me in the dark. Two of his buddies stood behind him. It was clear he wanted to fight. And I chose the fight as better than getting shot.

Jamie had more enthusiasm for the fight than I did but he was the smallest guy in the class and I was a head taller and thirty pounds heavier. I simply lay down on top of

him when he fell into a ditch. He said he had enough. Me too.

But at that moment a blinding light shined down on us. It was a flashlight beam. And there stood her father. It was clear to both Jamie and me that he was angry and mad as hell and not at all pleased that his daughter could arouse such passion from among her suitors.

"Both of you should be ashamed of yourselves," he said in a very loud voice. "Now both of you get up and get out. **Get out now!**"

I had always thought of her father as a mild-mannered man.

Jamie and I were better friends after our tussle in the ditch and I don't think either of us ever darkened her door again.

And Iris? She married Clement, a mild-mannered classmate of ours.

⁂

Don't Give Up! Happenings Can Still Happen

By Oswald Ragatz

Who dreamed up that image of the retiree sitting in a rocking chair on the veranda of a peaceful retirement home, dreamily reminiscing of bygone years when things were happening in an active live, a life filled with adventure and challenge? I wish to posit that this is not exactly the way it really is, not in the twenty-first century anyway.

Let me illustrate with one example of a happening that happened long after happenings are supposed to happen to an old geezer 81 years old. I was recovering from the trauma of my wife's memorial service when my daughter and son-in-law seriously embraced what they have come to consider a major responsibility in their busy lives, namely being certain that old Dad is not just sitting in the rocking chair on the porch mulling over morbid or maudlin memories of days of yore.

First I must explain about my son-in-law, Jack. For nineteen years he had been the chief fuel executive of Northwest Airlines. Basically this entailed his providing fuel at all airports around the world where Northwest planes land. This resulted in considerable travel to many cities of the world where **things happen**, especially in the Far East—Japan, Korea, Thailand, Singapore, etc. One of the perks of Jack's job was that wife Christa (our daughter) could travel free on Northwest to anywhere in the world. AND his parents and parents-in-law could travel first class at half price to any Northwest destination. This had resulted—back when things were supposed to happen—in some pretty exotic trips for us, to Japan, Korea and Thailand, for example. But now having passed that line between living and senility, I had presumed such exotic happenings were only to be dreamed about in rosy remembrances from the restraining restrictions of my rocking chair.

Ah, but not so! Jack, who is a world-class "make things happen" man, calls me to say that he has accrued two weeks of vacation time that he and Christa will tack on to his week of business in Tokyo, and I should go with them. Docile and obedient father-in-law that I am (and not about to pass up a good thing in spite of my advanced age), I found myself packing, not just travel clothes but dress-up clothes as well. I knew from previous trips to the Orient with Jack that in the East the elderly are held in great respect, and that I would no doubt be included in the numerous luncheons and dinners the oil companies would be hosting for Jack-san.

Northwest guzzles mega gallons of fuel, and the oil people, as well as the providers who transport fuel from storage tanks to the airports, are eager for Northwest contracts. So consequently, these suppliers of the necessities of air travel go all-out to curry favor with Northwest. Hence with Jack-san.

Limousines await arrival of the big man from the U.S., plus his hangers-on such as wife and in-laws. On our first visit to Tokyo, there were two such vehicles awaiting us, one for the passengers and one for the luggage.

After two weeks of shrines, temples, pearl divers, tea ceremonies, always with a driver/

Barbara Restle

guide at our beck and call, the bullet train from Kyoto deposited us in Tokyo, and Jack went into full business mode: meetings all day with the Japanese government (which has tight control over all that goes on at Norita airport), and a final gala dinner hosted by Shell Oil Japan.

Now these big shot oilmen never travel solo; there are always two or three minions as well as chauffeurs. Wives are seldom included, but in this case since Jack's wife was along, wives were also included in the festive dinner. There were three Americans and three Shell Oil men and their wives in the party. I was seated at the end of a long table, with Jack at my right, and across from me was the very attractive wife of Shell Oil Japan's President. I'm sure she was a trophy wife. She spoke very good English and had been a singer in a nightclub. (I don't know the Japanese term for *chanteuse*.)

Conversation was quite easy. Jack was chiefly involved with the oilmen, Christa at the other end of the table with two wives. Mrs. Shell Oil (I must call her that as I had no idea what her name was or what the protocol would be in addressing such an individual) was very interested in travel to America since she and their two twenty-something children were coming to American in the next month or so. Incidentally, their destinations were Las Vegas, San Francisco and New York—and she didn't have a clue as to the distances between these points of interest. Japanese cities all sort of run together.

So the long dinner was finally over, and Jack sidles up to me saying that they are going on to a Karaoke bar and would I like to go along. Christa wisely was going back to our hotel. Well, it sounded pretty racy, though I didn't

have a clue what to expect, so I ignored the fact that I was a senior citizen, presumably with judgment and caution, and I said yes. Shortly, we were whisked to the bright lights of the Ginza and deposited at a nondescript door on the street, then climbed single file up a long flight of stairs leading to a small entryway.

The room was surprisingly small, probably 12 by 40 feet. At one end was the bar, at the other end a single, wide table with circular seating on three sides, looking like a giant breakfast nook. Our party of eight, plus geisha-clad hostess, sat us as follows: hostess, me, Mrs. Shell Oil Japan, Jack, President of Shell Oil Japan, a wife, a minion, another wife, and another minion. Drinks were automatically served in large water glasses.

Hostess leaned over cozily, asking me to light her cigarette, which I did, but Hostess shortly realized that there was no action here and wafted away. Meanwhile, I realized that the large TV monitor hanging from the ceiling had lit up. A couple of minutes later came the booming voice of son-in-law Jack singing *Moon River*, following the words on the monitor.

Now at last I am getting to the point... During Jack's rendition of *Moon River*, I felt a hand moving seductively up my inner right thigh, Mrs. Shell Oil's hand! Now this seldom happened in my post-puberty youth, but I sort of remembered what one was supposed to do. However, at age 81, with her husband two seats away and Jack in between, it was not difficult to maintain a stance of cool, disinterested virtue during the remainder of the evening. I must admit that I was more bemused than confused throughout all of this. The somewhat active hand was never removed, incidentally. Thankfully, after everyone else had sung, it was decided it was time to leave.

While we awaited our limos, *femme fatale* sidled up to me saying, "I wish we had more time," then gave me a wet, unexpected kiss. At which point President of Shell Oil Japan strode over, took his wife firmly by the arm and piloted her into the limo. I looked at Jack, who had a smirk on this face, like the proverbial cat that has eaten a canary. I think the fink knew all along what was going on and had purposely set up his stuffy father-in-law and had enjoyed every minute of the happening. And, indeed, I consider it a **Happening**, sort of like a ride in a stunt plane that, after scaring your socks off, lands safely, no loss of life (or in this case, no loss of virtue), and the pilot has a smirk on his face. Later attempts to discuss this event with Jack were futile, resulting in his smug, amused look.

So the moral of this tale is to tell the elderly not to stick too tightly to that rocking chair. There is still a big world happening out there. At least take a look!

✳✳

After 41 years at Chairman of the Organ Department at Indiana University's School of Music, Oswald Ragatz has enjoyed twenty-three years of retirement, traveling, and writing mystery novels.

A Soviet Potato

By Barbara Restle

The train from Moscow to Leningrad was surely the same one that carried Russian soldiers during World War II. This was early November in 1978 and the weather in Moscow was heading for a long Russian winter. The train was chilly and during the journey I never took off my trench coat, wool beret and gloves. I boarded the train in the morning with arrival in Leningrad scheduled for early evening. Within an hour or so, I noticed that the leather boots I was wearing were dampening in standing water. No one else appeared to be bothered by this, so I did not question my travel companion Dmitri, my KGB-designated tour guide for the day. Apparently, this was all part of traveling by train in the Soviet Union.

We were seated in the rear of the train car, and I had a good view of my fellow travelers. I was the only tourist. In my well-traveled wrinkled trench coat I felt overdressed and knew that everyone could easily label me as a tourist. After several weeks traveling in the Soviet Union I was accustomed to move about as if invisible: no fleeting smiles or eye contact. The men in black suits, who exited the next door hotel room the exact same time that I left mine, shadowed me every day and I simply ignored them. They must have been bored, annoyed, even insulted with this daily surveillance.

After several hours, a young man in front of the train stood up, turned towards his fellow travelers, stretched out his arms over his head and said something that made people close to him respond with subdued friendly chatter. He was a robust young man, wearing rough farm clothes, his tousled blond hair framing a wide tanned face and his smile was that of a disarming innocent boy. The week I spent in Moscow, I saw very few smiles and never on the faces of the young. I thought it was possible this man was traveling with his family. He stepped out into the aisle and took something out of a canvas bag and showed it to people on his side of the aisle. At first I did not recognize what it was, only that it was quite large and bulky. The response from the passengers was one of surprise and pleasure. Soon the object was handed to all passengers on the left side of the train and when it was handed to me I saw that it was a potato. It was truly the largest potato I had ever seen in my life. It was almost as large as a football. I stood up, holding the potato in both hands, gave the young man a big smile, and handed it to the man sitting behind me. The potato was handed down the right side of the train and back to the young man.

I spoke to Dmitri and told him how impressed I was with the size of this specimen and how I wished I could talk to the young man and try to learn about his farming methods. Dmitri's response was a quick negative one. The journey was beginning to bore me and I needed diversion. The weather, as we moved closer to Leningrad, deteriorated into a minor snow storm and this was early November. I had been so cold in Moscow and I had prepared for traveling north by wearing flannel pajamas under my slacks. I now knew even this might not be warm enough.

After an hour or so I saw that the young man had opened the train door which led into the entryway of the train. Before Dmitri could stop me, I followed the young man out. He was smoking a cigarette. In English and with pantomime I informed him that his potato was truly the largest and most wonderful one I had ever seen. He responded with his generous open smile and said, "*Spacibo.*" (I thank you)

When I returned to my seat, Dmitri indicated that he did not approve of my following the young man. He was indeed acting like a stern disapproving teacher stuck with an intractable student.

The train slowed into the Leningrad terminal and everyone stood up and gathered their belongings. Then I saw the young man walk with determination toward me, hold out his hand and with slow, careful articulation said, "Cooperation and Friendship." His words were spoken with conviction; his broad smile contagious. I only had time to take off my beret, unpin one of my many travel emblems on my hat and hand it to him. He took my symbol of friendship and rapidly left the train. I wanted to know how he knew these perfectly pronounced words. He obviously had been taught them after I tried to communicate with him in English. Someone on this train spoke English, and had watched us and initiated the message of cooperation and friendship.

The crush of everyone leaving the train quickly separated us and I never saw him again. Standing on the platform, Dmitri angrily asked me what I had given the young man. He was clearly annoyed with me. The symbol of friendship I had given the young man was hard to explain to my KGB-designated tour guide. I finally said, "I'm a member of an organization and it is called DUCKS UNLIMITED." ⁂

A Seeing Eye Dog Honeymoon

By Lois Morris

Some experiences stay with you, and some memories you never forget. How many people can say that they have been a "Seeing Eye Dog" for a visually impaired couple on their honeymoon? I can. And I did it for a couple named Lee and Earl.

I knew Lee through what was known at the time as the New Jersey Reformatory for Women, in my position as assistant superintendent. The superintendent was a very progressive woman who had hired Lee, the first woman to graduate from the Columbia School of Social Work, as a social worker for the reformatory. It was a good experience for Lee, and a good experience for everyone involved. Working with Lee really brought out the best in everyone.

Lee and I became good friends over the course of her career at the reformatory. During that time, I also came to know her family, who were very nice people. I used to vacation with Lee each summer at the Jersey Shore. One summer Lee asked if her friend Earl could come along with us, and I said that was all right with me.

It turned out that the two had met over a talking book of *The Godfather*. Talking books, at that time, were common, and played on a phonograph. Earl was employed as a counselor for the New Jersey Commission for the Blind (Now the Commission for the Visually Impaired), and he found out through the Commission which lent talking books to the visually impaired, that Lee had its recording of *The Godfather*. Earl knew Lee already, and he didn't want to wait for her to return it—the novel was a very popular book at the time. So Earl got in touch with Lee, who recommended that he come over and listen to it with her. Well, *The Godfather* led to bigger and better things. They fell in love, were married, and the rest is history.

I went to their wedding, and afterward took them to their hotel in Newark in preparation for their honeymoon in Aruba. I had volunteered to be their seeing eye dog for their honeymoon—a week in Aruba—and though it would be quite an honor. Let me tell you the flight down was something else. Lee told me to alert the airline that the couple was visually impaired, and we really got the royal treatment which was new for me: the VIP lounge, goodies to eat, lots of attention from the airline and also the attendants on the plane.

And when we arrived in Aruba, it was like paradise. This was the 1960s before Aruba became overly commercialized. It had one casino and very few hotels, and it felt as if the newlyweds had the island to themselves for the week.

We stayed in a villa called the Divi Divi, named after the beautiful trees that populated the island. The Caribbean has nice calm water, so the two enjoyed basking in the sun and swimming in that cool green water. Lee and Earl appeared like all young lovers. They walked close and held hands, when they weren't holding mine to be led someplace. They were really a joy to be with.

At the beach, Lee would listen to the talking books she had packed for the trip, and I often worked crossword puzzles with Earl, who was quite good at them. He really had a sense for how grids were laid out, and how the words worked within them—he was very good. I would give him the clues, and he would give me the answers. Then he's ask, "Now what's going in the other direction?" And we'd work our way through the puzzle.

We always had good service from the cabana boys, who would bring towels and cold drinks to our chairs on the beach. I can remember one of the boys saying in the middle of the week, as he poked a finger at Earl, "My God! He no see either." The boy didn't realize that *both* of them were blind.

Although both Lee and Earl were born blind, they were very independent. They didn't rely on seeing eye dogs (except for me in Aruba), and were really capable people. And Lee wasn't afraid to step out on her own. I do remember that she said winter was the worst time of year because the snow deadened the sound and made it difficult to hear what was around her.

Well, we were like tourists in Aruba and explored the island in a broken-down taxi cab driven by a cabbie who spoke broken English. I would describe the island as we drove along. I did neglect to mention all the little animals and insects that inhabited the island. I did tell the newlyweds what we were passing and what a particular noise or scent was. Let me tell you, you haven't lived until you have had to describe a sunset to someone who has never seen it, how the wind blows over the island, or how beautifully Divi Divi trees bending in the breeze.

One memorable afternoon in town, the couple went shopping in a jewelry store. I described some of the jewelry in the cases, and Lee saw something she liked. When she "sees" something she likes, that means she liked my description of it. It was a necklace that really got her attention. And just as Earl was about to buy it for her, the shopkeeper announced that the store was closing for siesta. Can you imagine that, a siesta right in the middle of a sale? But it was siesta time, so forget about buying anything. Well, the couple came back, Earl bought the necklace for Lee and she adored it.

After the honeymoon, we kept in touch, and continued to vacation every year on the Jersey Shore. They have both passed now. It was a wonderful experience, and I am so glad that I met them, that we became such good friends, and that I could share that special time with them.

Barbara Restle

PART II

MEMORIES OF WARS

WORLD WAR II

KOREA

VIETNAM

FIRST DAY OF ARAB SPRING

Sooth'd with the sound, the King grew vain;

Fought all his battles o'er again;

And thrice he routed all his foes,

And thrice he slew the slain,

John Dryden

1631 -1700

Troop Train
December 1941

By June Keisler

Always I remember
The darkness, the rain
The fog-lost whistle
Of a mist-bound train;

Always the faces,
Indistinct, wet
The feet plodding past us—
I cannot forget!

Always the unending
Night, and the rain,
And the unceasing sound
Of the wheels of a train:

One last hard kiss;
Dry-eyed good-bye
Good-bye, tonight, beloved,
Wherever you lie.

September 2, 1945: Tokyo Bay

By Bernard Clayton, Jr.

A war that had been fought across the world finally came down to an American battleship, the Missouri, anchored peacefully in the enemy's home waters.

It was a perfect day for a surrender. Clear and cool, a delightful contrast to the heat and humidity of Manila, where I had been just three days before to join the Army advance unit into Japan.

I was among a group of fellow correspondents roused out at five o'clock for a brief breakfast in the Army mess and then driven to a dock in Yokohama to board the destroyer Murray for the seven-mile trip to the Missouri.

Aboard the destroyer we pretty much agreed—after having seen the terrible devastation caused by B-29 raids, that the atomic bombs were not needed to end the war. We had heard rumors in Manila that peace overtures by the Japanese through the Russians had begun in July and that surrender was only weeks away.

The Missouri was the centerpiece of the drama.

Aboard the battleship the deck officer noted that the bay was smooth as glass, without a ripple, and she was anchored in ten fathoms of water, mud bottom, and with 50 fathoms of chain to the starboard anchor.

Near the battleship, we off-loaded from the destroyer into smaller vessels and immediately found ourselves in a traffic jam of launches and gigs and barges full of admirals and generals and captains and colonels and war correspondents jockeying for positions at the ladders into the ship, to beat the nine o'clock deadline when the Japanese delegation was to come aboard.

Our small boat was waved off twice, and each time we approached I was in awe of the vastness of her broadside. From my tiny cockleshell she was enormous; a giant steel wall. The Stars and Stripes flying above the mainmast was the same flag that had flown over the Capitol in Washington the day Japan attacked Pearl Harbor. I could hear a military band somewhere on the ship rehearsing Anchors Aweigh.

It was on the third time around when a voice rang out from someplace high in the battleship.

"Hey, Bernie Clayton," a familiar voice boomed across the water. "General MacArthur welcomes you! . . . and I welcome you!"

Good lord, it was John Florea, a *LIFE* photographer and an old friend. I thought he was in Europe covering that war. But here he was. I should have known.

Once aboard, we were directed down passageways and up ladders until we came out on the navigation deck looking down on the table where General of the Army Douglas MacArthur and his official party were to stand when the Japanese delegation of 11 men, diplomats and officers came aboard.

When the Japanese walked to the table, covered and skirted with green felt cloth, the entire ship grew silent. Not a sound.

General MacArthur motioned the Japanese Foreign Minister, Mamoru Shigemitsu, to the table. Wearing the formal garb of diplomats—top hat, swallow-tail coat, striped pants, ascot, and white gloves—he hobbled forward on his cane, placing his hat and his gloves on the edge of the table. His signature was in Japanese, made with the delicate strokes as though painting.

The Allies signed.

MacArthur rose to the microphones. "Let us pray peace be now restored in the world and God will preserve it always."

"These proceedings are now closed."

It was over!

At that instant a remarkable thing happened. More than 800 carrier-based aircraft that had been circling out of sight and sound during the ceremony now came low in formation over the Missouri. Also above them circled dozens of B-29 Super fortresses.

Everyone aboard the battleship—admirals and generals and sailors and soldiers and correspondents—stood transfixed by a sight that would never be repeated. Clouds of planes—fighters and bombers—filled the sky. The thunder and din of thousands of engines was as fearsome as it was thrilling.

The second highlight of my day was mundane. It was a tooth that had been aching all week. I walked down to a troop transport alongside the wharf and introduced myself to the ship's dentist. One yank and out it came. A quick and painless extraction. He even threw in a double shot of Old Grandad whiskey.

I walked back toward the shabby old hotel where correspondents were staying, feeling not too good. I dreaded the mess, where the rancid smell of fish from the old hotel kitchen overpowered everything that our mess cooks could put together.

Happily at the moment a half dozen of my fellow correspondents asked me if I wanted to go with them to see if they could promote a dinner on a Navy troop ship that had just brought in the First Calvary Division of occupation troops.

It was glorious!

The ship was celebrating the end of the war big time: turkey, dressing, mashed potatoes, gravy, peas, cranberry sauce, bread and butter, and huge platters of three kinds of ice cream.

I decided then and there that in my next war the Navy was the way to go.

It was the end of a perfect day.

Bernard Clayton, Jr., Bloomington author and a Meadowood resident, was a war correspondent for Time-Life Magazine in the Pacific theater for most of World War II. He was assigned by the magazines first to the Pacific fleet headquarters at Pearl Harbor and then to the MacArthur command in Manila, and finally Tokyo. He is best known, however, as the author of several best-selling cookbooks.

Growing Up Jewish in a Nazi World

By Luise David

When I was 10 years old, I transferred to a new school, a special girls' high school called the Lyceum. My old school had been only a block away from the apartment house we lived in. Now I had to walk almost to the other side of town. I liked it a lot better in the new school. There were new surroundings, different subjects to learn, all kinds of girls from other parts of town. I started to read more; I found out that learning could be fun. My grades, mediocre before, began to improve. I studied English and French and realized I had a good year for languages. At long last I had discovered something I could do well.

Something was happening to me I did not understand. I was changing in some ways. Alice, my stepmother, whom I adored, had told me I would become a woman, but it had made no impression. One morning in May, like many times before, I walked to school through the underpass, up the hill to a grove of lilac bushes bursting into bloom in the morning sunshine. The blossoms on the tip of each cluster shimmered pink and mauve in the sun; the closed, deep purple buds glistened. Intoxicated by the strong perfume, I saw it all as if for the first time. I felt as if my chest would burst and my skin explodes. The whole world changed for me that morning.

I was at once both happy and sad. I knew that from now on I would feel joy as well as sorrow more deeply. I vowed not to talk to anyone about this; it would be my secret.

I walked to school as if in a daze, but noticing everything I passed with sharpened awareness.

Alice seemed to sense the change and too realize that I was no longer a child. It was then that she told me about Franciscka's suicide. Franziska was my birth mother, who had died in 1919. Alice also told me that she thought that Father had some extramarital affairs. I was shocked. I may have seemed ready to be her confidante, but I was her stepdaughter, not her friend! I did not let on how it affected me. I committed everything she told me to memory to mull over later. I realized then that Alice lacked the proper instincts about some things; she had hoped to draw me closer but instead had created a gulf between us.

I have always wondered if a disenchantment such as this could happen during adolescence between a birthmother and her own daughter. I do not really think so. In any case, abruptly, my childhood had ended.

(I want to add here that I never believed that my father had extramarital affairs. He was so totally wrapped up in his patients' lives that there was no time left to give in to temptations of this kind. My father, the well—reputed doctor, was also a very ethical person.)

Once I graduated from the Lyceum, I enrolled in the three-year course offered to girls at the Nürnberg Labenwolfschule. It meant traveling by streetcar from the further Plarrer, the end station, to a station in Nürnberg near my school. This course I was to take would entitle me to matriculate at any German university to study to become a pediatrician. But the Nazi world we lived in was to change my plans. New laws were constantly issued to curtail the careers of Jews and alienate Jews, making them feel like second-class citizens.

In my second year at this school, another new law made it mandatory to begin each school day with the standard greeting, "Heil Hitler." I quit school that very day.

My feeling about religion had not increased since I had graduated with fairly good grades from the Lyceum. When I took the time to come to a conclusion about God, I could not help but think that he was no longer there for Jewish people. How could he be, when so many Jews were killed, hunted down by Nazis, often tortured? Later in life, when I began reading books about the Holocaust, I took comfort in the fact that one of the best-known survivors of the Holocaust, Elie Wiesel, wrote that he found it unbelievable that the God he had learned to love and believe in could let such a horrible fate happen not only to Jews, but to gypsies, socialists, Russians, anybody whom the Nazis deemed to be an enemy of the Third Reich.

My parents had many talks to discuss how I could get more education before I would emigrate. In 1933 and 1934, most Jewish parents felt that their young ones had to leave Germany and get to a safe haven abroad, while they themselves hoped to remain until the Nazi madness blew over. After many talks at home, Father and Mother told me that I should take the opportunity to learn more skills that I could use to get a job in a foreign country. As my brother was already in Jerusalem, I should prepare to do housework and light agriculture so I could work in a

kibbutz, where new immigrants to the Holy Land could work for the common good.

I was registered in a housekeeping school near Munich, where I could learn these skills. I would also learn Hebrew, as the ancient language was not used in the new country Jews had hoped to build. The school I was to attend offered courses to give students the needed skills.

When I arrived a few weeks later at Wolfratshausen, south of Munich, where this school was located, the countryside and the buildings in which we lived looked lovely. I liked to be among girls of my age. That day I met my roommate, Leni Carlebach. She and I proved to be well matched. The one big difference between us was that she was Orthodox, while I had been brought up as a Reformed Jew.

I became aware of Leni's deep faith and had great respect for her total commitment to live a life according to Jewish laws. When school began officially, we were in the same class and learned light agriculture. Kosher cooking, raising chickens and how to milk a cow. There were no classes on the Sabbath. Leni called on all of us to come to the big lawn on Saturday afternoons and study Hebrew by reading the Bible with her. With her knowledge and interpretation, the text now made sense. I am sure that I was not the only one who had a religious epiphany that summer.

Life for Jews still in Germany took a turn for the worse that we should all have expected, but did not. Instead of going to Palestine, I ended up in Hamburg to work for one of the teachers from Wolfratshausen. She had left the housekeeping school. Elizabeth Mirabeauhad applied for a job in the Hamburg Jewish community to become manager of the Jewish orphanage for girls. She offered me a job without pay in the orphanage to come and help as an extra person, where I would learn on the job so I could use childcare skills wherever I would end up once I emigrated. I accepted the job. Instead of a salary I would get room and board. The supervision of this place was in the hands of the Orthodox Jewish congregation. My training in the boarding school had prepared me well. Learning more about childcare would be fine. It was now 1935.

My life took another strange turn when my father met a young man on a train in Bavaria who was to become my husband in 1936. I began to think again that there must be a God after all who had one of his angels looking out for me.

The life I have led, has taken me to strange places and introduced me to lots of people. It has also taken many of my loved ones from me much too early and under terrible circumstances. I will muddle along for as long as I live; I was given the best that life can offer: loving children and grandchildren—and now two great-grandchildren. May God bless them all.

Luise David was born in Bavaria. After emigrating with her husband, Frank, and her son, Carl Wolfgang (now a professor of physical chemistry at the University of Connecticut), to America. She worked as a claims adjuster in New York's garment district. Her daughter, Susan Gubar, is Distinguished Professor of English at Indiana University. David is the author of a memoir, "How We Survived."

                Barbara Restle

Captain John and the Egg Woman

An excerpt from a book
By Rosetta Knox

[Ed. Note: In 1945 Rosetta Knox worked in the resistance movement in the Italian Alps. Rosetta was in her mid-twenties, and in spite of the horrors of the war, she never forget her femininity nor her humanity.]

———————————

A little old woman comes to the camp. She is as dark and dry as a smoked anchovy. Dressed in a rusty black cotton dress and apron that reach to her ankles, she wears on her feet a pair of men's shoes without laces, on her head a black cotton kerchief. She stops, curiously looks around her at the circle of card players, at the men sitting around, at the iron pot simmering on the fire. She takes her time, then she asks, "Is Commander Gek here?"

Gek gets to his feet, smiling, benevolent. "I am Gek. But commander I am not. And so, good woman, what can I do for you?"

"Signor Gek, the Englishman, the tall blond man, you know him? But yes, you know him, he is here with you, in the camp. You see, Signor Gek, the Englishman comes every day to my house to buy eggs, but when it comes to paying . . ."

"But, my good woman, we can't pay for the eggs Captain John eats. You know that, don't you?"

"No, No, that's not why I have come. You see, the English gentleman pays every time with a thousand lire note, and Signor Commander, I don't have the change for a thousand lire, I will never have the change. But you, you can make the change for a thousand lire, Signor Commander?"

"That I can do, *nonna*, that I can do." Gek smiles, places his arm across her shoulders, pushes her toward the path. "Go, *nonna*, go, I will take care of it." And he sends her off reassured. Gek and all of us know that Captain John not only loves the old woman's eggs, but her hens as well and courts them assiduously. He lures them away from the farmyard with handfuls of corn, and takes them for walks out of sight of the farmhouse. The hens follow him, pecking at the corn. At a safe distance the captain falls flat on his stomach, makes enticing sounds in English while the hens peck and cackle, then they squawk when he throws a lasso. The hens are in no danger. Captain John is not an expert with the lasso. They have finished pecking the corn and make their way home, back to the hen house to make the eggs that the captain will buy. Gek has not told the old woman this—perhaps out of consideration for Captain John or to spare the old woman.

Rosetta Knox was trained to teach English to Italian students in Italy. She ended up teaching English, Italian and French to American students in America.

The Training of a World War II Pilot

By Eugene A. Merrell

My interest in flying began after Pearl Harbor when a low flying military plane circled the campus of Arizona State Teachers College. The pilot waved his arm and from the reaction of the girls nearby I figured that being a pilot must have its advantages. That summer I traveled to Santa Fe, New Mexico, where I qualified for Aviation Cadet Training and enlisted on August 19, 1942. I was given a deferment to finish college but that never happened. The following April, I was aboard a troop train going to Wichita Falls, Texas, for basic military training. I spent the next month learning basic military skills and living on the flight line in Hanger 4. There were about 1,500 of us living in that hanger. The transition from civilian life to military life was not easy. When I completed basic training I was classified as an Aviation Student and transferred to the College Training Detachment (CTD) at Texas A&M University.

The commander, a product of the West Point Military Academy, was a strict, no-nonsense Captain. Except for hazing, his belief in the West Point method of training was reflected throughout the detachment. Our instructors were a mixture of well-qualified college professors and military officers. Classes, physical training and studying kept us busy from the time of Reveille until the welcome notes of Taps were sounded. Breaks were few and far between, but once in a while nice things happened.

One Saturday afternoon I volunteered for an unspecified detail. We changed into clean uniforms and marched to the train station. Only then were we told that we were to meet an incoming group of people who would need help with their luggage. We were not told that it was an organized group of young ladies associated with the USO at Houston. Nor were we told that they were to be guests of the detachment at our party that night. When the train stopped and beautiful ladies started down those steps, the cadets came alive and eagerly made their selection of who needed help the most. I was a little slow on the uptake and was almost left empty-handed. As luck would have it, one of those bundles from heaven was also a little slow. When she appeared, it was obvious that she needed help, and I was there. On the way to the dorm, she asked how to get to the dance. I told her I didn't know how to tell her, but I could come by and take her there. She accepted my offer and smiled. I was very happy to have a date for that night.

She was a very good dancer. It is to be noted that the chaperones from the USO and the detachment officers were very observant and took their responsibilities seriously. Nevertheless, it was a great party. A few weeks later, our class was on its way to the Classification Center at San Antonio, Texas.

At the Classification Center, I went through a suspense-filled month of testing to determine if I met the mental and physical standards established for pilot training. It was common knowledge that, at best, only three out of five of us would complete the Aviation Cadet program. Several in our group were medically disqualified. Others, unable to pass the standards set for pilots, were earmarked for training as Navigators or

Barbara Restle

Bombardiers. Fortunately, I was among those who qualified for pilot training.

There were four phases in the pilot training program, each one lasting nine weeks. They were Preflight, Primary, Basic and Advanced. Preflight concentrated on academics and physical training and discipline. At Primary we continued our studies and were taught the fundamentals of flying in a PT-19, a monoplane with open cockpits and a crude system for pilot-to-student communication. Not long after I had been cleared for solo flight I nearly lost my life. Disregarding any need for instruction or authority I took it upon myself to try some acrobatic maneuvers.

As might be expected, I soon lost control of the aircraft. Losing altitude rapidly I had no idea how to recover. With disaster staring me in the face and only a few seconds left to live I instinctively did something I know not what, that brought the aircraft under control.

Almost in a state of shock, I returned to the base determined to quit. My instructor met me on the ramp, listened to my story and then literally forced me to get back in the cockpit to finish the period. During take-off my confidence returned. That experience taught me the importance of learning my own limitations and respecting the limitations of the airplanes I would be flying. I owe that instructor a debt I can never repay. Others were not so lucky.

Basic flight training at Enid Army Air Field included flying in a BT-13, a large more powerful airplane. It was an unforgiving airplane and one that was difficult to fly. The focus was on acrobatics, formation and instrument flying. Mistakes could be fatal.

There were also other pitfalls that could cause serious problems.

Foolishly, I violated the unwritten rule that cadets were not to date any of the secretaries in the Cadet Headquarters. A golden opportunity presented itself and I took it. When the news got around, I became the victim of subtle harassment by the officers. I began to wonder if I would be around much longer. When I left Enid Army Air Field my appreciation for the need to follow rules and regulations was much greater. When the class left for Advanced, I was among those selected to attend training in multi-engine aircraft. Although I had wanted to become a fighter pilot I knew that I was lucky to still be in the program. Our ranks were thinning rapidly.

Transitioning into multi-engine aircraft was not easy. The UC-78 had two engines and more than twice as many instruments to monitor. The emergency procedures were more complicated and instrument flying was stressed. Instrument flying continued to be my weakest area. When I had finished taking my last check-ride I was sure I had failed. The flight examiner looked up from his notes and said: "You did okay, you passed." I didn't argue the point. My cadet days ended June 27, 1944, when large formations of base personnel and lower class cadets honored the graduating class of 44-F by passing in review. My mother and my sweetheart pinned the gold bars of a second lieutenant on my collar. The secretary from Enid smiled as she pinned those coveted silver wings above the left pocket of my uniform.

My first assignment as an officer was to Hondo Army Air Field where I was attached to a training unit. This is where I came to terms with instrument flying. After I had learned local procedures and had demonstrated my competence, I was permitted to fly navigator training missions. Pilots averaged over 100 flying hours a month. Single pilots were usually scheduled for the night, weekend, and holiday missions. My social life continued to be very limited.

World War II was about over when Hondo switched over to training B-29 Flight Engineers. Within a year I had married the secretary from Enid and had been assigned to five different bases including spending 22 miserable days on a troop ship bound for the Philippine Islands. There I was first exposed to the ravages of a brutal war. When I reported to Headquarters 13th Air Force I became Chief of Personnel Classification and Audit Team. Mine was a traveling team. I enjoyed the assignment but was discouraged by the dependent travel situation. I applied for Release from Active Duty and within six months, I was separated from the service at Camp Beale, California. I met up with my beloved wife in Oklahoma City. With the exception of one year, I continued to fly military aircraft as a Reserve Officer. I returned to active duty on April 15, 1953 and remained until retirement in 1978.

*
**

Barbara Restle

A Glimpse of the Past

By Eugene A. Merrell

When I parked in my driveway that cold day in February 1953, I had no idea I would soon be making a decision that would change my life forever. My wife, Colleen, nearly eight months pregnant, met me at the door with a letter from the U.S. Air Force offering me an opportunity to return to active duty in a voluntary status. We discussed our options and both agreed that this was our opportunity to return to the life we liked best. Two weeks after the birth of our son, I was *enroute* to Lackland Air force Base, Texas, for processing.

Things did not turn out quite as expected. Instead of an assignment to a flying unit in Korea, I was assigned to Carswell AFB where I would become the third pilot on the crew of the huge B-36 bomber. When I reported for duty it was obvious that I had too much rank and too much flying time to fill that position. Fortunately, and to the relief of the squadron commander, there was an opening for me as Adjutant of the 7th Field Maintenance Squadron.

Although I did not realize it at the time, that assignment was the best thing that could have happened to me. It put me on a career path that led to some very interesting staff assignments in the Administrative, Education, Operations and Personnel career fields. Still, I regretted that my opportunity for combat experiences would be limited. My chances of becoming a hero were pretty slim. Individually, my accomplishments seemed unimportant, yet when I added them together, my opinion changed.

During the first ten years, I held routine administrative positions and flew missions while based in Korea, the Philippine Islands and the United States.

When the rapid expansion of the airlift capability caused a shortage of C-130 pilots, I returned to the cockpit on a full time basis. When I completed combat crew training, I was transferred to the 772nd Troop Carrier Squadron as an Aircraft Commander and given a crew. The copilot and navigator were young and just out of school. The Flight Mechanic and Loadmaster were experienced. We had to be trained to fly in all known environments. We had to become proficient at flying dangerously low over the target area and using a tail hook or parachute to pull the cargo from the rear of the aircraft. We had to learn how to take off from unimproved runways as short as 2500 feet. We took our training seriously and were among the first new crews to become "Combat Ready." I have landed on tundra and a frozen lake in Alaska, in the deserts of California and scores of other places in North and South America, including the airport at La Paz, Bolivia, elevation 13,000 feet. The C-130 was the best airplane that I have ever flown.

All too soon, I was transferred to headquarters where I became the Wing Mobility Officer. My first priority became that of developing a Mobility Plan for the rapid deployment of up to 75 aircraft including the equipment and supplies necessary to support 30 days of operations. A few months after the plan was published, I was given ten days notice to report to Travis AFB for transportation to Vietnam.

My tour in Vietnam was a busy one. Shortly before my tour was over, my name appeared on a list of officers who were to submit an application for an AFROTC assignment. I objected and was overruled. I wanted back into Tactical Airlift. Weeks later I found out that I would be going to Indiana University.

Three days after leaving Saigon, I joined my family at Langley AFB, Virginia. We were soon on our way to Bloomington, Indiana, to make a courtesy call and look for a house. I found the detachment commander at the old stadium on 10th Street where they were holding the annual President's Parade. It was there I met I.U. President Elvis Stahr and learned that I was to become the Professor of Aerospace Studies. After we had located a place to live, we spent the rest of my leave getting reacquainted. Our quality time ended the morning the North American van containing our household goods arrived as I was leaving for Maxwell AFB to attend the Air Force Academic Instructors Course at the Air University.

The sixties and early seventies were difficult times for those in the ROTC program. The cadets and officers became targets for those faculty members and students who were against the war in Vietnam. The activists were busy. Abusive and non-violent confrontations were a daily occurrence. There were no serious incidents, but the cadets and officers were verbally abused. It was known that I had recently returned from Vietnam.

In spite of this, the ROTC instructors took their jobs seriously. They were more than teachers; they were counselors, confidants, task masters, and a second father to each and every student. One of their objectives was to increase the image of the cadet corps to a level that was above criticism. Both the instructors and cadets achieved almost 100 percent participation in the campus blood drives, ushering at games and conducting successful clothing and toy drives for needy children. More importantly, they generally were good students and their conduct reflected favorably upon themselves and the University. Fortunately, President Stahr, Chancellor Wells, and most of the senior members of the faculty and staff recognized the value of educating tomorrow's military leaders and blocked the many efforts that were made to bar the detachment from the campus. While there, I received the Bronze Star and Air Medal for service in Vietnam and was promoted to the rank of Lieutenant Colonel. My departure for a special assignment at Andrews AFB was without fanfare or regret. ⁎⁎

World War II Pigeoneer

By Bill Christiansen

I was drafted into the U.S. Army in October, 1941. I tried to enlist in the Air Corps, but I couldn't pass the eye test. I was sent to Camp Wolters, Texas, for my 13 weeks of basic training. After training we were assigned to various units to bring them up to full strength.

I was first sent to the 108th Regiment of the 27th Infantry Division which was the New York National Guard. In April 1942 we were shipped to the island of Maui to fortify the island against possible Japanese attack.

About two months later the Army, in order to create more fighting units, changed the configuration of divisions. The 27th Division which is called a "square division" was changed to a triangular division, with three regiments instead of four. My regiment was the "odd man out" and we joined the 40th Division which was the California National Guard.

While I was in the hospital with pneumonia, I was visited by Lt. Sedgwick who said he was forming an intelligence and reconnaissance platoon in Army Headquarters Company and that he would like me to be part of it. I jumped at the chance and transferred the same day.

As I became acquainted with my new friends I discovered that we had a "pigeoneer" Ed Barkoviac, complete with large portable cage and about six or seven birds. I was genuinely puzzled by this fact until I discovered we were operating under a "table of organization" that was still in effect from World War I.

As the war progressed, we "visited" other islands including Guadalcanal, finally ending up on the island of New Britain which was in the Bismarck Archipelago. We were on one end of the island and the Japanese naval base at Rabal at the other. We were told that Rabal was the largest Japanese naval base in the Pacific outside Japan. This was in November of 1944. We still had our pigeoneer.

Our goal was to invade the island of New Ireland which was much closer to Rabal. About 4 a.m. there was a ruckus at Headquarters. No shots were fired so we were not being invaded. When we reached the site, we found that an eight-foot python had stuck its head through the chicken wire, swallowed one bird and couldn't get out.

When the pigeoneer checked up on his carrier pigeons the next morning all the cages were empty. The night before the officers had squab for dinner.

MacArthur, in his wisdom, canceled the invasion of New Ireland. Instead we became part of the invasion army that hit the island of Luzon on January 9, 1945.

***

Not my Time

By Bernard Clayton Jr.

*   *   *

As a war correspondent in the Pacific theater for Time-Life magazines during World War II, I often flew to the mainland to report to my editors in New York. This time I was aboard a Navy PB2y3: a flying boat.

It happened in the middle of the night and in the middle of the Pacific. I was alone, smoking—couldn't sleep—seated on one of the benches below and behind the flight deck and forward of the quarters where the dozen or so other passengers, all Navy personnel, were asleep. The captain was in his bunk in a small compartment just below the flight deck. A short ladder connected the two. The copilot was alone at the helm. The plane was flying on automatic pilot.

Suddenly the plane, which was flying at about 6,000 feet, nosed into a steep dive. I sat transfixed and pinned by the force of the dive against the bulkhead behind my seat. I could see the co-pilot, his hands on the steering column, his feet up and pushing against the instrument panel—pulling back with all the strength in his body to get control of the plane. It was deathly still except for the terrible sound of the air rushing over the wings and through the struts. No yells. No screams. Just silent prayers.

The plane was in a terrifying dive into the ocean and it couldn't be stopped, or so it seemed. The door to the officer's quarters burst open, and out crawled the captain, clad only in his skivvies, fighting powerful G force. He clutched the door sill and the guard rail and fought his way up the ladder to the flight deck. He pulled himself into his seat, grabbed the other steering yoke, jammed his feet against the instrument panel and, pulling with the copilot, tried desperately to control the plane.

My prayer, as I recall, was a simple one: Lord, don't let the steel cables connected to the control surfaces break!

It was strange. While I realized that I was about to be killed, I also knew that the pilots might succeed and I willed them to *pull, pull, pull.* So be it. There was nothing I could do. It seemed an eternity before I sensed the plane begin to respond and slowly come out of its dive.

Barbara Restle

The plane leveled off near the water and began a slow climb. The two men dropped their feet to the deck. The captain reached over and gave the copilot a pat on the shoulder. They had done it. It was over. I felt drained.

There was a celebration of sorts among the grateful passengers over coffee and Coke when the captain came down to explain that the automatic pilot which suddenly malfunctioning had been filled with faulty fluid in Australia. While it had been drained and replaced at Pearl Harbor Naval Air Station, obviously someone had done a poor flushing job. From this point on, the plane would have to be flown hands-on by a pilot at the controls. On long flights, this is a boring, tedious and a tiring job that pilots hate. The plane had been flying at about 150 knots per hours.

When it went into the dive, it reached an estimated 250 knots, the captain said. He said had he crashed, the plane would have been reported missing since he had no opportunity during the struggle to send a radio distress signal to locate us.

The plane would never have been found in the vastness of the Pacific. I didn't ask how close we came to crashing, but the ocean seemed only a few feet away when I looked out of the window to see the waves close by, rolling and breaking in the moonlight.

I guess I didn't want to know.

A Trip to London

By John Brogneaux

It was my lot to be assigned as Armed Guard Commander aboard the gasoline tanker S.S. Pasqual transporting a million gallons of high-octant gasoline to supply U.S. Air Forces in England, Ireland and Scotland.

My job—along with my crew of 36 gunners and loaders, three radiomen, three signalmen, a junior gunnery officer and a communication officer—was the defense of the ship and the Merchant Marine crew. The Merchant Marines were the unsung heroes of World War II.

They operated the ship in very hazardous waters. They were well paid, but had no military standing. All were civilians, many older men served as captains and ships officers. All had extensive sea experience. The crews were supplemented with officers and men trained at the various Merchant Marine academies.

History shows that between 400 and 500 of these ships were sunk with most of their crews!

We sailed from New York harbor and formed a convoy with 15 other ships, carrying fuel, planes, troops and all kinds of supplies as well as oil and gasoline. We proceeded on a zigzag course, with three destroyer escorts sweeping with sonar to find the U-boats lurking under water.

We arrived in Gourock, Scotland, in ten days, after losing one of the gasoline tankers and all the crew to a U-boat attack. We were diverted to Loch Ewe for further orders in Northern Scotland. We knew that the convoys going to Murmansk, Russia, were formed here for the extremely hazardous trip.

The Boarding Officer came aboard with our orders to proceed to London. It was a surprise to me and I told him that I didn't know high-octane tankers were sent down the North Sea to London. His answer: "If you get through, we will have established a route." Quite a challenge!

We sailed down the North Sea following the marker buoys in the deep channel. We stopped at Port Leith at Edinburgh, Scotland, and were joined by a small escort vessel manned by the British. After a hundred miles of sailing, we noticed that our gyro compass was malfunctioning, so the ship's captain and I decided to anchor the ship until repairs could be made.

As the fog set in, our man in the bow watch reported a floating mine was approaching. It was too close to attempt firing it. The tide was running rather rapidly, which created a large wake and kept the mine about four feet away from the ship. It floated 520 feet along side and disappeared. So we escaped that one!

After we repaired our compass, we proceeded down to the mouth of the River Thames. A ship ahead of us was preparing to pass through the subnets when it was torpedoed. As it started to sink we received a message by flashing light to come along side and help. Knowing that subs were around, we were loathe to do this—since we would probably be blown up. So we suggested they launch their lifeboats and rafts since land was near.

Stopping a tanker at that time and place would probably have been sheer suicide.

We proceeded through the subnets and sailed up the River Thames to Thames Haven to discharge our cargo. It was mandatory to take my voyage reports to the port office in London, so I boarded a train, and got off at Charing Cross Station to carry out my mission.

While there, we had a buzz bomb attack launched by the Nazis from Denmark. So I was advised to go down into the subways for safety. I went down about 75 feet and saw hundreds of people there. So I decided to take my chances on the topside rather than the possibility of being buried alive. I soon caught a train back to Thames Haven where we had completed discharging our cargo. We filled our tank with water, sailed up the North Sea to Scotland, joined a convoy and sailed back to New York Harbor. Subs didn't bother our empty ships.

Editor's note: John P. Brogneaux was a well—known high school athletic coach, a Navy officer during World War II and also an Indiana University professor.

My Story

By Ardis Jerden

As I was finishing high school in Mt. Morris, Michigan, in 1940, war clouds were hovering over England and Europe. I entered General Motors Institute (GMI) in Flint, Michigan, in September of 1940, pursuing a business course. At GMI, engineering students would alternate two months of academic study with two months at a General Motors plant somewhere in the United States. On December 7, 1941, Japan bombed our naval facility at Pearl Harbor, and President Franklin D. Roosevelt and Congress declared the United States was at war with Japan. Soon we would be at war with Italy and Germany too. Immediately, all automotive and aircraft plants geared up for defense manufacturing. After graduating from GMI, I was employed by Buick Motor Division—first in a secretarial pool typing defense contracts, then as a secretary in personnel, and finally as a secretary to five executives in the aluminum foundry. I worked at Buick until I was married.

I met my husband-to-be (Charles Cleatis Jerden—known as "Cleat") when I was a junior in high school. We attended our high school prom and marched together at Commencement. We were also in several plays and musicals together.

All men between the ages of 18 and 30 had to register with the draft board to see if they were eligible to serve in the military, and if they qualified physically and mentally, they could choose to enlist in the various branches of service; Naval Air Force, Army Air Force,

Marine Air Force and Army Intelligence. All the young men hoped to become officers. Cleat qualified for the Army Air Force and left in January, 1942. He trained in various stages of pilot training in Kentucky, Florida and Georgia, where he received his pilot's wings and became a lieutenant in the Army Air Force. He trained to fly B-25 bombers with a five-man crew.

Cleat and I married in August, 1944. After our ten-day honeymoon in Northern Michigan, he was assigned to Columbia, South Carolina, for further training and to get a crew assignment. I joined him there for five months. Fort Jackson Artillery base was also located in Columbia, so housing was at a premium. We rented a bedroom, shared a bathroom with three other military couples, and had to go to restaurants for all our meals. At this time, my husband was enduring night flying training, so I would have dinner with other military wives. Mr. and Mrs. Pennell, our landlords, were lovely people whose only son was lost at sea on an aircraft carrier.

My husband and I went back to Michigan in December, where he said goodbye at my parent's home and left on a train and embarked for overseas to the 5th Air Force Stationed in the Philippines. Before returning home in January, 1946, he completed 41 missions and survived a mid-air collision with another plane. The tail of his B-25 was sheared off and the crew dumped everything out of the plane in flight. After successfully landing at the American base, the plane was scrapped. Cleat and crew were sent to Australia for rest and rehabilitation for one month. I didn't know any of this until he returned, as all military letters were censored so that the enemy would not learn information from them.

Barbara Restle

All of America was filled with patriotism—we wanted to win the war and have our sons and husbands return home. Many women went to work in factories as there was a shortage of men. There was a song written at the time called "Rosie the Riveter" about women working in defense jobs. Families who had sons in service would display cards in their windows with silver stars—or gold stars if their sons had died in the war. We had many forms of rationing—we were issued food stamps to purchase meat, gasoline, and shoes. There was no extra gasoline for pleasure trips—only for mileage to work. We were issued two shoe stamps a year. I wrote to my mother when I was in South Carolina, begging her to find an extra shoe stamp from someone, as my shoes were about to fall off my feet.

When I returned to Michigan, I discovered I was pregnant, so I stayed with my parents while my husband was gone. Charles Alan Jerden was born on August 10, 1945. The war ended while I was in the hospital, and all the nurses and doctors were celebrating. I wasn't sure my husband was alive. My mother sent him a telegram informing him that he was the father of a son.

When the war was over, all the military men who were overseas had to wait for transportation home. Cleat was on Okinawa at the time and decided not to fly, but came home on a Navy ship. It took five months! I met him in Detroit on January 11, 1946, and barely recognized my husband: he was so thin and tanned. Since he served in the South Pacific, he was taking Atabrine tablets as s deterrent to malaria.

Building of houses had stopped during the war, so it was difficult to find a place to live.

We bought a small house in Mt. Morris, and Cleat worked as a manager of a local bank. A daughter, Susan Elaine Jerden, was born October 1, 1947.

The GI Bill was passed and signed by President Franklin Roosevelt in 1945, enabling all servicemen to enroll in college and have tuition, books, etc. subsidized by the government, along with $125 for monthly subsistence allowance.

We sold our home in September 1948 and moved to Ann Arbor where Cleat enrolled at the University of Michigan in the Liberal Arts program. We lived at Portage Lake until we could move to an apartment near campus. The University apartments were filled with returning servicemen and their families, and we had many potluck dinners shared among residents. Our apartment rent was $85 out of our $125. I worked for a year as secretary to the Dean of Pharmacy before becoming a stay-at-home mom. ⁂

Vacation Time in the Army Air Corps

By John W. Fox

For two and a half of the five years that I spent in the Army Air Corps in World War II, I was stationed in India. Our unit airlifted a multi-national infantry column into central Burma and provided air support for their operations against the Japanese. For much of that time we were based in a rural jungle area where living conditions were primitive. In addition the monsoon, rains arrive about May and continue to October. This stopped just about all ground—based military activity so we were moved back to a location in the flat desert-like area of India west of Calcutta. These climatic conditions also meant that the reason for our unit's existence evaporated . . . no mission . . . lots of free time.

With lots of time, energy, and airplanes in an interesting country it was easy to think of places to explore . . . such as Kashmir, up in the Himalayas . . . a day's flight away. Kashmir has to be one of the world's more spectacular recreation areas. Located about 200 miles north of flat, steamy New Delhi, India at an altitude of about 5500 feet, the Vale of Kashmir is centered on a sizable lake (Nagin Bagh) with miles of canals. It is also surrounded by snow-capped mountain peaks in the range of 25,000 feet. You live on a houseboat anchored on the lake. Servants to prepare the food and carry out your every wish live on a smaller houseboat attached to the stern of your boat. So, off we went to Kashmir. There was no airport in Kashmir in the 1940's but the Maharajah's polo field worked just fine.

The capital town of Srinagar had plenty of taxies to get us to the water's edge. Then there were many water taxies . . . small, flat, low-sided boats called *shikaras* to carry people around the city's canals and to the lake. You sort of lay back on old automobile cushions under a fabric roof, with side curtains giving a bit of privacy. In back were four guys with heart-shaped paddles who sang little musical chants as they propelled you along and while you dangled your hand in the water.

The *shikaras* all had expressive names. When you arrived at the dock you had to make a choice between "Field Marshal Montgomery With Full Spring Seats" or "Big Careless Rapture" or "Fulla Beans," "Cautious Amorist" or "Happy England," and many others. Once on your houseboat there was plenty of room to relax in comfortable surroundings, lie on the top deck in the sun, or go swimming, play cards or whatever. You could go shopping in town at Joyful Jacob the Jeweler or Walnut Willie the Woodcarver or Cheerful Chippendale. You had to see the Shalimar Gardens. And there was a continuous parade of merchants in *shikaras* coming by your houseboat, offering flowers, gorgeous embroidered garments, carved ivory and teak and other merchandise.

Barbara Restle

Houseboat in Srinagar, Kashmir

Downtown at Nedous Hotel there was dancing almost every night. At these dances you would see men in uniform from Europe, Asia, South Africa—various parts of the world (lots of gold braid and shoulder-boards), although American and British garb dominated. And the girls were mostly American and British. There was one notable exception, however, that I remember. There were two young women, very attractive and obviously Indian but certainly westernized. These girls, it so happened, were the daughters of the Nizam who was the ruler of Hyderabad—princesses, no less. They were having a good time dancing just like all the other young people there. And the young men were responding too, cutting in on them just as they cut in on other girls. Later, one of our young officers was told about their being royalty and he was astonished; "Hell, I was giving her a big snow job about West Virginia when I danced with her!" The princesses certainly added interest to Srinagar. They drove around the town in a white Buick convertible, top down with a license plate, "Hyderabad 1." All the American men, jeep-weary, watched, and turned green with envy.

You could also take a day trip to the town around Gulmarg at about 1000 feet higher altitude, where there was also a golf course.

There was day trip to view some frozen lakes at 14,000 feet. These trips were on horseback with you riding the horse and the horse's owner running alongside. You felt a long way away from the war. ✳✳

Water taxis, or *shikaras*, in Kashmir

A Line in the Sand

By Walter Taylor

In the Fall of 1947 I was assigned to the 42nd Engineer Battalion of the Army's 24th Corps. We were stationed in prefabricated barracks on a sandy field near Yung Dung Po, Korea, a sprawling suburb of Seoul. We Americans served as post guards and drivers for an aging fleet of tow-and-a-half ton trucks which had to be double-clutched every time the gears were shifted.

At this point the Army was still segregated, and my unit was all white. Down the street from us was a black unit which was assigned to drive the same trucks. They referred to themselves as "the double-clutching so-and-so's." You may give this euphemism your own interpretation.

We became familiar with these men: worked out of the same motor pool, played sports with them, etc. But the real integration of the armed services under President Truman was to come much later.

Most days we spent our off-duty hours boozing in the service club. The double-clutchers had their own service club. Soon we began to see some black faces in our club, and word was spread of an agreement between the two clubs that they were open to everyone.

One night several of us decided to walk down to the double-clutchers' club. We were welcomed and drinks were passed around. They seemed glad to talk to us—nothing special, just good fellowship. But the differences between the two groups were soon obvious.

My group—indeed most of our unit—consisted of draftees or short-timers like myself; at age twenty I was one of the oldest. In a year, most of us would be back in civilian life. The people we were talking to were several years older and they were serving five-year enlistments. Their maturity (as compared to ours) was obvious. But a kind of sadness hung over the place—at least for me. These men had joined the Army because it offered a security that the segregated United States did not offer. One or two of them seemed simply lost. One man who wanted to be a physician had memorized all the bones in the human body, and would be happy to recite them for you. It was clear that this man was never going to have a chance for a medical degree.

This friendly exchange went on for some weeks. Then one night in our service club a young white guy from Virginia spoiled it all. He was not a big man, a Private First Class, sandy-haired, somewhat in his cups. He became known as "The Rebel." He wanted it known that he did not want black men at the next table in what he considered *his* service club. This went on for some forty-five minutes.

People were taking sides. Somebody sent down to the double-clutchers' headquarters for help. It showed up in the person of their top sergeant. He was the biggest man I had ever seen. Not tall, just *big*. He approached it all very calmly. In the silence that fell when he entered, he asked the Rebel to step outside and discuss the matter. All of us trooped out and surrounded the two of them. There was of course a strict regulation against a private

Barbara Restle

attacking a sergeant. The double-clutchers' top kick did not seem too worried. With his combat boot he drew a line in the sand between himself and the Rebel. "If you've got a problem," he said, "just step across this line."

The Rebel made no move to cross the line.

The sergeant turned to the rest of us and asked if anybody else wanted to cross the line. No one wanted to.

"All right," he said, "you are all welcome any time to come to our club. But I'm not letting any of our guys come back here where they're not welcome." And he turned and escorted his people back to their compound.

I'm not sure why, but I never went back to the double-clutchers' service club. I don't know that anyone else from our group did. It was only later that I realized that the line in the sand had more than one meaning. Yes, the sergeant had made his point and he had taken care of his own. But there was a paradox there. The line in the sand meant that he had returned us to the segregated Army we had known. The Rebel had won after all.

The following spring I was discharged and returned to my home in segregated Mississippi. I did not know then that President Truman was going to integrate the armed forces. Or that the double-clutchers, long-termers all, were going to have a war to fight before two more years had passed.

**

My Teachable Moments in an Ominous World

By Miriam Rosenzweig

In April 1933, shortly before my eighth birthday, my family took a train from Munich, where we lived, to Vienna. That wasn't unusual because my mother's parents, brothers and their families all lived in Vienna, and we had often gone there for visits. But after a while, I realized that this trip was different. My parents never talked about going home, and I began asking questions about our return. My mother explained that a very bad man, named Hitler, who wanted to harm us, had become the ruler of Germany. Munich was part of Germany, and we would never go back.

That's a lot to swallow for an eight-year-old. But, as it turned out, my transition to my new surroundings was easy and enjoyable. I had cousins, who were my age, and there was a lot of visiting and playing together, and it made them feel important to educate me in the ways of Vienna and about our family. One cousin, who was a few years older than I, told me that our grandfather was the inventor of plywood, and that he made plywood in a large factory in Vienna. Several years passed before I learned that this was a vast exaggeration of my grandfather's accomplishments. He did have a plywood factory in the city, but he did not invent the process by which it is made. Laminated wood had been found in the tombs of Egyptian pharaohs and there are 17th century records, showing the French and English working wood along the general principles of plywood: the gluing together of several sheets of wood with the grain running crosswise from one sheet to next. My grandfather's contributions were some time-saving improvements in the gluing process. His factory thrived, and he became a wealthy man.

When he reached late middle age, my grandfather's memory began to face. His condition worsened rapidly, and at that time he gave the factory to his four children, three sons and my mother. The brothers assumed management, and not wanting a silent partner, they bought my mother's portion of the factory from her. This infusion propelled us into a somewhat higher rung of the middle class and its life style.

We lived in a large apartment in an affluent part of the city. It had ample space to house my parents, their four children, my father's library, a cook and a maid. Our maid Paula was young, pretty and gentle. One of her duties was to get me off to school every morning. School started at eight and was a half hour's walk from our house. That meant I had to get up early, and my parents were nowhere in sight at that time. Paula combed and braided my long hair, gave me breakfast and prepared the mid-morning snack I took to school. She was there for me when my mother was not, and I felt close to her. One day, I returned from school to find Paula in tears and sobbing "I didn't do it." My mother had found sheets missing from the linen closet and accused Paula of stealing them. Her suspicions were not absurd. It was a common occurrence for the service staff to steal linen, silver and china from their employers. They sold these items through fences, often their boyfriends. I don't know what rules of evidence my mother used to accuse Paula and to find her guilty, but she was gone the next day. I was deeply shaken and unhappy about this turn of events, and in my heart I felt Paula was innocent.

My grandparents too, lived in a large apartment, and they owned a summer house in an outlying district of the city. By the time we arrived in Vienna, my grandfather's mental capacities had vanished completely. I remember him as a friendly old man with a bushy mustache, who never said anything that made sense. It was my grandmother who reigned as queen of the household. Members of the close and extended family spent much time at their house. I remember sitting at a long dining room table where lots of people had gathered for the mid-day meal, or for afternoon coffee. The meals were excellent and the baked goods, accompanying coffee, fabulous. Cooking and baking was done by a cook, who had long been employed by my grandparents. The meals were served by a maid. On some occasions, when the adults were engaged in lively conversation, and there were no suitable playmates present, I brought my own entertainment. One day, I brought Charles and Mary Lamb's "Tales from Shakespeare," translated into German. While I was reading, the maid looked over my shoulder and saw the word "Shakespeare." She was unfamiliar with it and began sounding it out: "S-ha-kes-pe-a-re." I told her it was pronounced Shakespeare. Then she said: "You are so young, and already you know more than I will ever know." The profound sadness in her voice stayed with me for a long time and led me to a new insight into the human condition. Not everyone is satisfied with their station in life.

My grandparents' summer home had an attached servants' apartment for the caretaker and his family. They saw to it that the house was clean and habitable at all times and the grounds cared for. When our family arrived in Vienna, we stayed there until we found our apartment. The place was paradise for young children. There was a large lawn, where my older sister taught us acrobatic tricks. Some areas had shrubbery, ideal for playing hide-and-seek, and there was a plum tree I could climb in season to pick fruit that went directly from tree to mouth.

During the summer months, my grandparents lived there in the same way as they did in the city. The housekeeping help moved had with them, and many relatives dropped in for coffee or dinner. My grandmother had an older brother Alfred, in his eighties when I knew him. At that time, I began wondering about the characteristics of old age. I had observed that I never saw my grandparents jump and that their hands and arms sometimes trembled. Was that the case with all old people? One day, when Alfred was visiting, I cornered him and said: "Uncle Alfred, since you are old, I bet you can't jump anymore." He told me to jump as high as I could. Then he jumped higher than I. That was baffling, but I continued the test and said: "I bet you can't hold your arm out straight without trembling." My great-uncle, who was a slender, wiry little man, extended his arm ramrod straight without the slightest tremor. I was perplexed. Are there no reliable characteristics of old age? Whenever I thought of this incident in later years, I was embarrassed. How could I possibly have been so rude? But I also remember the smile on Alfred's face and I suspected that he was highly amused.

In April 1938, shortly before my 13th birthday and exactly five years after our exodus from Munich, my family was on the run once again. This time, I was old enough to know why. Germany had annexed Austria, and Hitler was after us again. When one of my uncles was incarcerated, the danger became immediate and real. We left a few weeks later. After spending some months in Switzerland, awaiting our immigration visas, we took a boat to New York, where we settled. This time integration into my new surroundings was not so easy. I had to learn a new language, which made school difficult, and we did not enjoy the welcoming arms of our extended family, whose members had now become dispersed across three continents. My acculturation came slowly, and sometimes I feel that it is still a work in progress. ✺

Barbara Restle

Two Small Vignettes from Life in India

By Ella Wade Fox

Vignette #1

[Ondal is a tiny village in the province of Bengal, north of Calcutta, site of a large American Air Base]

One morning I heard music and wondering its source, I stepped outside my basha. Across the rice paddies I saw an Indian man approaching. He was dressed in his native garb, a bit ragged and wearing the usual large turban on his head. Across his shoulder he carried a long pole with a shallow basket hanging from each end. As he approached, several other Americans gathered, also summoned by his playing on his pipe, a flute-like instrument.

When he reached our group, he squatted on the ground placing the baskets in front of him. He uncovered one basket and then resumed his music. As he played, a large cobra raised its head about 18 inches above the basket. The Indian swayed back and forth in tempo with his tune and the cobra, with its hood extended, followed this action perfectly.

Here we stood, watching the performance of a storied Indian Snake Charmer. Our little group of Americans were transfixed—not really hypnotized but certainly enchanted.

Vignette #2

[Ranikhet, a Hill Station in northern India lies on the border of Tibet]

Our Red Cross Club for enlisted men was located in these beautiful foothills of the Himalayas. The G.I.'s would spend two weeks of R and R in Ranikher and our club provided a great program of activity for them. We had an English girl, Molly Wagstaff, a resident of the town of Ranikher on our staff. Her knowledge of the area was a great asset to us: the leper colony we visited, the local Swami, Panther's pool—a destination for horseback rides and picnics. One evening Molly invited two of us Red Cross girls to her home as her dinner guests. What a treat to spend an evening in a private home. After a delicious meal prepared by her Burmese chef, we sat on her front porch, enjoying the clear and cool mountain air and the peacefulness her home provided.

While we chatted, Molly's old dog, Chini, lay on the steps in front of us, apparently dozing. We looked out on a large lawn with many trees. They were nut tress of some sort and their fruit was on the ground everywhere. A whole "herd" of small monkeys covered the ground, enjoying a feast of these nuts. Suddenly Chini came to life and charged up through the lawn, sending the monkeys dashing up into the trees to safety. No damage was intended. It was a game. From their perch these little monkeys were shouting bad things at the old dog. Chini strolled back to resume his nap on the porch step. We could see, however, that he "napped" with one eye slightly open. At last the monkeys descended from their treetop perches and very warily went back to their feasting on the nuts. Once they were engrossed in their meal, Chini suddenly came to life again and charged up the lawn—a repeat performance, with the monkeys dashing up into the trees, chattering furiously and scolding Chini. This little charade went on several times, giving us great entertainment. It was a novel sight for us Americans.

A small aside: these monkeys were so different from the ones we saw in Bengal, which were very large and rather intimidating; they never approached us and we never invited them to do so. These very small fellows here in the mountains were friendly to a fault and very mischievous. I have a wonderful picture of one youngster who had stolen a can of Planter's Peanuts from our cottage porch. He sat there on the porch roof holding the can and enjoying its contents. ✲✲

Barbara Restle

My Indian Initiation

By Ella Wade Fox

[July 1944 in a Red Cross Hostel
On Park Street Calcutta, India]

I am vaguely aware of lying in a pool of perspiration, burning with fever, my entire body hurting intensely, so that it is impossible to move. Am I dying? The last occupant of this bed was also a Red Cross girl. She had died. In fact, her clothes are still in the armoire. I had to push them aside so I could hang up my things when I unpacked.

Am I already dead? Am I in a casket? Are these the walls of a wooden casket I am looking at? The fear brings me to full consciousness. Whew. The "walls" are only the brown mosquito netting draped on the four sides of my bed. I slip once more into blessed unconsciousness.

Next I waken to listen for some sign of human life in this dormitory room. Everyone has left to go to work. The only sounds come in strange wails from the music school next door. This is music? I hear the soft pad of our sweet little ayah's bare feet as she crosses the room to bring me a cup of tea. "Chia, Memsahib?" Oh no. The very thought of having to swallow something makes me nauseated. Again I slip into unconsciousness.

And then I feel myself being lifted by strong arms and laid on a gurney. Now into an ambulance and on to the army hospital. Here the two doctors agree: a classic case of Dengue Fever . . . the raging fever and aching.

And oh, do I hurt! It's no wonder the British call it "break-bone fever"!

Ten days earlier in Bombay, when I stepped ashore from the troopship George M. Randall, I evidently tangled with a mosquito. Why did he pick on me? Leaving the ship, there were 6,000 troops, 30 other Red Cross girls and 20 nurses. The nasty insect could have feasted on them.

This was not the type of "experience" I'd anticipated when I joined the Red Cross . . . and it certainly would not be included in my letters home. (Don't worry my mother!) Home! I am in far-off Indiana—half way around the world.)

*
**

Culture Shock in India

By Ella Fox

Culture Shock? In July of 1944, more than 6,000 Americans debarking from their troop ship onto the docks of Bombay reacted with more than "culture shock." It was disbelief—awe—disgust . . . ! The sights and smells were certainly foreign to anything we had ever experienced. Coolies, both men and women, worked unloading ships in the harbor. They carried unbelievable loads, always on their heads! People were asleep (or dying) on the streets and sidewalks. And the beggars were everywhere, mostly children. "Bahkshees, Sahib. No momma, no poppa. Bahkshees, Sahib!"

Calcutta. Here were the Grand and Great Eastern Hotels with their fine dining and Firpos, a favorite restaurant for Americans, and the Calcutta Swimming Club with both indoor and outdoor pools and lots of bearers to bring you a sandwich or drink as you basked in the sun. These were a great contrast to the extreme poverty that existed outside these walls. The streets were a "movie set." You could see everything. White sacred cows roamed the streets, into the train station, the market place. Again, coolies trotted through the streets carrying all sort of things: six men trotted in unison carrying a piano on their heads; another foursome carried a bedstead with a body *enroute* to the burning *ghats* (funeral pyres); one man bore a big basket of live white chickens; another a basket of beautiful flowers—always on their

heads, no hands! People washed themselves at a water spigot in the street, brushed their teeth, shaved. Lots of rickshaws, gharries (horse-drawn carriages), and taxis of 1920 vintage driven by fierce-looking Sikhs.

I guess the most startling sight was seeing the women (the untouchables) who walked the streets scooping up the droppings of the ever-present cows. They filled their baskets, again carried on their heads. Returning to their mud huts, they made the contents of the baskets into "patties" which they plastered on the outside walls of their huts. When the patties dried, the women peeled them off and used them as fuel for their household fires. This was a common custom as firewood was scarce.

Off to my first assignment as a staff member of the Red Cross Club. It was at Ondal, about 120 miles up into Bengal. Living quarters were very primitive, to put it mildly. We girls, like the officers, lived in a basha. This meant we had rooms rather than a barracks like the enlisted men. My roommate was a girl who had come over on the same ship with me and we were good friends. Like the officers, we had a bearer since there were no accommodations on base for female servants. Our bearer took care of our clothes, dusted our room, and made our beds—pretty luxurious!

The basha was a long cement building with a thatched roof. It was divided into about six rooms, with two girls living in each. There was a burlap ceiling in the room to keep the thatch dust from falling down on us. That space between the burlap and the roof was a favorite nesting place for rats. At night they

Barbara Restle

would descend, looking for any morsels of food. One night I heard my perfume bottles being knocked over on my dressing table. I shined my flashlight around to determine the source of the noise. A huge rat was chewing on my leather manicure case. It made me glad to have the "security" of my mosquito netting tucked tightly around my bed.

There was a long aisle down the length of the basha and across from each room was a bathroom. No real plumbing. We brushed our teeth with water from our canteen. There was a huge tank on top of the basha and that provided water for our showers. In winter the water was frigid and in the summer, heated by the sun, it was so hot we could barely stand under it.

The bearer always took our laundry to the dhobi (a man belonging to a caste of launderers) who pounded the clothes on rocks to clean them and then, during the monsoon season, had to dry them indoors in his own large basha. The dhobi had no electricity. His iron was filled with coals, yet his perfect ironing was impressive. His fire was made from (you guessed it) the same fuel we saw being collected in Calcutta. It was cow dung. We girls tried doing our own bit of laundry whenever possible.

We kept very busy in our Red Cross Club, located near the enlisted men's barracks.

Boredom was a hazard for men at Ondal. This was the largest service base for planes before flying "the Hump," the treacherous Himalayas. After working on the planes, there was no recreation for the men except for activities in our Club. We had a canteen where they could come for coffee, etc., a small library where they could read or write letters,

a large living room with a stage at the end for visiting entertainment (some of which the men themselves provided), a large room with a ping pong table and a dance floor where I taught everything from jitterbug to tap! We had tours of the local Maharajah's palace and sometimes he would bring out his elephant and offer rides. We visited the local Tata Steel Mill and tried to find other spots of interest.

Occasionally we were able to gather enough women for a dance. They were usually Anglo-Indian girls who came well-chaperoned by many family members. And we would recruit girls from other Red Cross Clubs. The dances were the activity the men enjoyed most.

On the night of the Big Dance, the G.I.s would arrive all crisply starched in their fresh khakis, looking very handsome. And the dancing began. As the night wore on, the jitterbugging in the Indian heat and humidity had everyone's khakis melting. A faint aroma arose. It was the dhobi's fire fuel. Ah yes, shades of the "sacred cow's" contribution. But nobody cared. The party went on. We girls tried to name the "fragrance." Certainly not Chanel #5. Perhaps Sewer #6? ⚜

Tourism in Syria and the Arab Spring

By Rosemary Messick

Motives for tourism vary. In my case the desire to visit Syria grew with friendship. Knowing Brazilians of Syrian descent and hearing their family stories, admiring their drive to succeed and appreciating their cuisine combined to increase my interest in visiting Syria. Also, the fact that my friends and I speak Portuguese, their second language after Arabic, made Middle Eastern travel much less daunting. For years our group nibbled around the edges of the Arab world. We visited Morocco, Egypt, Tunisia, Lebanon, but never Syria, as it was considered too risky. Further, as an American, a travel visa was not possible for me since the United States had no diplomatic relations with Syria after the 1967 war with our ally, Israel.

The situation changed. The Obama administration re-established diplomatic relations with Syria. I would be able to get a visa. Tours to Syria began to be marketed from various European countries. It seemed that, at last, the time had come to realize our long-deferred trip. The idea of traveling to Syria moved from talk among my travel companions to putting down deposits on a tour. I had six months to prepare. I ordered all the guidebooks on Syria that Amazon had. My neighbor at Meadowood, Jean Herrmann, loaned me the Arabic textbook she had used while living in that part of the world. I could make neither heads nor tails of it. I had somewhat better luck listening to a CD from Berlitz while ignoring the Arabic script. I read history from scholarly books. Since my formal education about the Middle East was limited to early Christianity and the Crusades, I had a lot of ground to cover. Of course, current events since 9/11 had remedied my ignorance somewhat. Recent events certainly did not recommend tourism, but I continued to be stubbornly curious. I departed in September, 2010 from Indianapolis and my friends left from Sao Paulo, Brazil.

I realized I was crossing a cultural divide when lunch on the Air France flight from Paris to Damascus was served. Pasted on the stretch-wrap tray was a message: "Air France guarantees that this meal does not contain pork," in English, French and Arabic. A middle-aged Christian couple who shared the row with me was returning to Syria after 30 years living in Montreal. They reacted to the guarantee by smiling and positive head shaking. Damascus airport dates from the 1950s, but was very clean. The road to the hotel was newly paved. The late afternoon scene was sand—sand and dusky mountains backlit by the setting sun. Our hotel had the only green grass we were to see—an empty golf course with irrigation fountains at full flow and no golfers. Nor were there swimmers in the large pool even though the temperature was in the 90s. The new tourist hotel was ostentatiously decorated with large chandeliers hanging from a three-story ceiling, lots of stucco decoration incised in wall borders, huge Persian-style carpets on tile floors and large overstuffed divans. Few visitors were in sight. From our fifth floor rooms we could see feeble lights through the hazy air that must have been Damascus. Several miles separated the tourist hotel from the city.

Barbara Restle

Next morning a small bus was waiting for us in front of the hotel before the appointed hour. Our guide, Suiel, was careful to greet each of us and to see that our bags were stored properly. We were lucky. Throughout the tour he was efficient and careful to visit every itinerary item while providing copious narration in excellent Spanish. (The group of 17 was a mixture of Spaniards, Argentineans, Brazilians and me.) Over two days we toured Damascus monuments, museums, and the great mosque and but did not have enough time in the bazaar. Original walls surround the old city, claimed to be the oldest city in the world. Our bus was too large to enter the narrow lanes of the old city. Shops were full of goods and people. We stayed together, fearing never to be found if we strayed. We could have stayed days and not seen it all, or bought enough!

Then we headed east nearly all day through the desert headed for the Syrian City of Palmyra. We were traveling on well-paved roads over an ancient silk road formerly traversed only by camels. Occasionally I would spot sheep grazing on I knew not what, with a lone shepherd tending them. Bedouin tents were not far from the flock. An old pick-up truck was parked near the tents. Our rest stop, "The Bagdad Cafe", had outhouse-style toilets. The tea and coffee bar was powered by a generator fueled by a hose running from a barrel of oil standing in the open desert. Palmyra emerged from the desert. The green of the date palm oasis was muted by centuries of dust. Palmyra is surrounded by ruins of civilizations older than Greece. Touring them on foot in the 100-degree afternoon heat was an endurance test. That evening we strolled the streets of Palmyra, eating dates and enjoying the water canals. The city seemed mellow. Perhaps the mood came from the presence of water and the dusty green of the palms.

Ruins of Temple Bel in Palmyra, Syria

Returning east and heading north toward the agricultural region, we were bound for Syria's second city, Aleppo. On the way, the air conditioning on the bus quit. We were passing through Hama, a large, dusty monochromatic city which was closed down in observance of Ramadan. The driver discovered an open garage and a mechanic who vowed he could fix the problem.

We had traveled all morning with only one stop. We did not know how long we might be waiting for the repair. It was hot. There were no shops or restrooms in view. The men found places for relieving themselves. We women were left to persevere. I informed Suiel that I was beyond perseverance. He said to follow him and we entered an alley. He knocked at a gate to a small cinderblock dwelling. A traditionally dressed woman answered and immediately motioned us to enter. In Arabic Suiel explained my situation. I gratefully entered the home mentally prepared for a squatting-over the hole-in-the—floor experience. But No! This humble home had a tiled bathroom with sink, toilet and shower stall and a full bucket of water with a plastic cup for dipping water into the toilet and another by the sink!

When I opened the bathroom door the lady of the house seated me in the living room and served me freshly made coffee. Next she ushered in two older women who with the help of gestures and pictures, I learned were her mother and mother-law. Each carried a tray with small dishes of nuts, dried fruit and sweets for me to try.

Another knock came. The guide appeared with the rest of the women on the tour. This sent the ladies of the house scurrying back to the kitchen to prepare more coffee and snacks. There weren't enough chairs for us.

Soon the men on our tour found us and were also served. By then the husband and two children joined us. Pictures were taken, and e-mail addresses exchanged without benefit of a common language. I am sure the family was relieved when Suiel came to announce that the bus was repaired. I am also sure the family was proud of maintaining their culture of generosity to strangers.

This experience was not on the itinerary. Others like it followed, convincing us that Syrians of all classes were eager for foreign contact, but with restraint and dignity. However, we had the feeling that limits were always there, but we were not sure whether they were due to language barriers or to the strangeness and novelty of tourists in their midst. We found the large posters of the al Assads that decorated many buildings and the entrance/exit points to each and every city oppressive. Sueil was very careful to point out to us the many housing projects, roads, hospitals, and public offices given by the al Assads to the nation. Surprisingly, newpapers and magazines were not available in Arabic or English.

Still, we saw no beggars anywhere we traveled, or homeless or people with untreated illnesses. People appeared clean and carefully dressed and did not appear to be hungry. We were universally treated with courtesy and hospitality. Merchants did not hassle us to buy. Meals in restaurants were ample, delicious and very reasonably priced. We never sensed threat to our security, nor were we manhandled while in the crowded bazaars. No one was robbed or cheated. I learned quickly that religion was not discussed. I began to conclude that given the history of religious strife in Syria, perhaps the religious issue was best handled by ignoring the subject. We had visited numerous early Christian sites as well as famous, active mosques while learning nothing about current sectarian relations except that they were not to be discussed and that religious identification was not condoned. So we left Syria better acquainted with its ancient history than with its contemporary life.

Between our return from Syria in October 2010 and April 2011, we witnessed on television the amazing, nearly peaceful insurrections in Tunisia and Egypt. Arab Spring began. The effect of the demonstrations finally reached Syria in May. Now I recognize how little I had understood of what I had been seeing while a tourist in Syria. My Brazilian friends had lived through a dictatorship in Brazil and been raised by parents who left Syria in the early 1900s for economic and religious reasons. Even so, they tended not to doubt what we thought we were seeing—that Syrians were content with a regime that was moderating and becoming more open. We all wanted to feel that times were going to improve.

Now we know that perhaps as much as one-fifth of the population in Syria is employed by the regime to spy and report on the rest. We learn that in order to have employment, to have a paying job, young men stay in the military. We know that the circle around the al Assads control the economy and that most of the al Assads' minority religious sect, the Alawites, control the military and secret service and that they will shoot and kill their own people to maintain power, while declaring that they are actually battling terrorist gangs. I am not sorry to have been an innocent abroad. The experience helps me understand more about current world affairs and makes my heart go out to the people hoping that they survive to win greater freedom and opportunity, while keeping their sense of dignity, hospitality, and cultural pride. ⁂

PART III

POEMS

WORDS SWEET

AS HONEY FROM HIS

LIPS DISTILLED

WRITTEN BY HOMER

XANTIPPE

By Robin Black-Schaffer

Oh spare some pity
For poor Xantippe!
She wasn't wise
And she wasn't witty;

The neighbors envied
Her life of ease
As the wife of the famous
Socrates—

Who'd come home for dinner
Five hours late,
And push the cold food
Around on his plate,

Saying: "What must a famous
Philosopher do
To get a warm supper
Out of you?"

Then to the agora
To chat with his cronies.
Said she: 'Since you're going,
Bring home some bolognas."

Two days late he returned
Empty-handed and pursed
The Neighbors were shocked
At how Xantippe cursed.
Oh, reader, have pity
On poor old Xantippe,
Who was—as aforesaid
Not wise and not witty . . . .

But many a wife
From that day to the present
Understands why Xantippe
Was sometimes unpleasant!

SPIDER

By Nancy Seward Taylor

I watch you not go off the frame.

You stay inside.

Why do you impale yourself there?

One limb going off, the other in?

You just hang suspended.

Do I suspend myself in such ecstasy?

HOPE

By Ledford Carter

When the world's woes wind
their web
    To trap us,
    Slap us,
    And make us test our
    Sanity,
    We scream and roar
Which hurts even more;
    We bomb and kill
    Till the land is still
    To celebrate our vanity.

When such animal urges
become tame
And we learn to use our
brain,
    Then we see hope for
    humanity

After Bedtime Snack Thoughts

By Ledford Carter

My world is spinning fast. Grab that thought.
Much longer will it last? Stretch it, push it, twist it.
Of all the things I do, See what emerges.
I much prefer the new. True, it may remain a glob,
Yet drawing treasures best discarded.
     from my memories well Yet, on occasion it transforms
is a favored occupation. to a thing of beauty that gives joy
And turning them into stories to tell or fresh insight on that curious event
     brings me great elation. called Life. ✻
When no longer can I write,
I'll just dream day and night. ✻

Barbara Restle

The Metronome of Time

By Luise David

The metronome of time keeps ticking;
It is not heard by child or youth.
But in middle years' stressful moments
We notice its every-present beat.
Anguish, sickness, death—remind us—and
We listen, let its click come through
      the dissonance of sorrow;
A loved one dies—mortality, a word no more, is real.
We must go on, shut out the ticking.
Fading—it is inaudible again.
In moments brief did it command attention,
Forcing withdrawal from the world's reality—
And we hear glimpsed—
      thought we understood
The eternal cycle—life and death
      doing their dance.
Old age approaches, the beat is steady—audible now
Sounding a welcome accompaniment
      to the music of life.
It comforts, warns—bidding old age:
Consider what lies ahead—
      what must be left behind.

***

I Am Money

By Beth Van Vorst Gray

I am money,
Green, silver and copper
Bearing visages of America's past:
Jackson, Jefferson, Washington.
Laureates of government and glory,
Wielding power of the stability in my world.

I am money.
Once made only on demand with
Gold or silver to back me up,
I now recreate myself.
Moving from one hand to another.
Credit cards, bank notes
Promissory notes
Interest compounded daily.

I am money.
On computer-borne wings
I cross international borders,
Becoming red, pink, yellow
And fiesta blue in Mexico: brown, taupe
and purple
In Japan. Am I me?
Are they me? How do we know?
E pluribus unum?

I am money.
I have built cathedrals,
Paved highways, educated children,
Created whole civilizations
And founded great cities.
Paid for great art, music and literature,
Healed the sick and fed the poor.

I am money.
I have destroyed countries with war,
Paid for the annihilation of entire races,
Created weapons that can destroy the world,
Ruined good men and women in hot
pursuit of me.
A false god to those who worship me.

I am money.
Flowing like an everlasting fountain to the
Moguls,
A difficult and wearisome crop for most.
Like Janus, the two-faced god,
I always have two faces.
You choose. ✳

Barbara Restle

Reality

By Rod Ludlow

I stood alone on a clear dark night
High above the sleeping city
And gazed at the stars scattered like
      diamonds
Across the black velvet of the sky.
Their sparkling brilliance appeared to be
Just a touch away.
I reached out my eager arms
To draw their beauty to my heart
But found them far beyond my reach,
Like you.

No One Weeps But the Widowed Spring

By Esther Gaber

The clouds spoke at the wedding
Of the old man Winter
And the child Bride Spring.
"Tis not a good match,"
Said one to another,
"He's aged and worn;
She's young and so timid."

But nature had her way
And they were wed.
The old man knew
His days were few,
And took his bride
On a thousand-mile ride
For a honeymoon.

The whole land knew
He would live a while longer.
The clouds (punished for their gossip)
Turned large and black,
Then spread the land with ice and snow.

The last cold blast
Was Winter's end.
No one weeps but the widowed Spring.

All the flowers will attend
When Spring gives birth
And orphaned Summer enters in.

Barbara Restle

Haiku: Selections

Small roadside daisy,
Exposed to the whims of man,
Bravely lifts her head.

Red and golden leaves
Tumbling in the autumn winds
Carpet my reverie.

Wild, rushing waters
Overflow the river banks.
Dreams are swept away.

The black and white nuthatch
At home on a suit-filled log.
Can dine upside down.

—Elaine Lethem

Grandfather's Knee

By Robert Bayer

Securely on my grandfather's knee
I fingered the gold fobs he wore
From Odd Fellows, the Masons, the
 Moose, and the Elks.
I searched for the Juicy Fruit
Always buried in his left vest pocket.
With his thick white hair and apple
cheeks
He always seemed surprised at my
 discovery.

He took me blue gill fishing every
summer.
In Fall, we'd explore his sweet
 smelling orchard,
And go to farmer's market
Where he'd talk with Joe, the Market
 Master
We ate pickled herring and Limburger
 cheese

I can still smell his bay rum fragrance
When I sat securely on his knee
And watched the rings of smoke
He'd blow, floating gentle,
Like his smile.

Barbara Restle

ELEGY FOR MOM

By Robert Bayer

In an antiseptic nursing home
Outside Fort Wayne Indiana,
Tied in your wheelchair
Like a gunny sack of coal,
Forgotten by your god,
You mutely sat staring at nothing.
Held captive in your black-hole world
you looked but did not see.
Listened but did not hear
Did you sense death
Perched nearby patiently waiting?
When I took your hand,
Was it a tear I saw in your eye?
And upon departing,
When I looked at you.
For the last time.
Did you know you slowly raised
Your hand and waived?
Your last unforgettable gift of love.

Sleep

By Elisabeth Savich

Come Sweet sleep
    Visit me
Lift my weary body up
    Where pain is barred
Come gentle sleep
    Flood my mind
And wash out
    The worries of the day
Come renewing sleep
    Revive my troubled
    spirit
With the cool breeze
    From your ocean of
    reserve
Come penetrating sleep
    Reach my soul
Mend it
    And make it whole.

*
**

Barbara Restle

Twilight Years

By Basil Wentworth

When I was young (about a hundred years
Age, it seems), each day went by so fast
(And full of that day's business) that is passed
Without a thought about my Twilight Years.
There wasn't time or energy for fears.
The Golden Days would come, I knew, at last,
But each day's glorious memories amassed—
And so I lived each day, and shed no tears.
And now those days are on me. They are still
Well-filled with life. That youth of long ago
Was right—he must have sensed somehow
I need not worry: life and love would fill
Each day as always. So these days, I know,
Aren't Twilight Years or Golden Years—just now. ⁂

The Roving Reporter

By Virginia Gest

Once I saw a calligraphy exhibit in
London, and I wrote down these lines to remember:

———————————————————

O Lord, grant that we may not be like
cornflakes: lightweight, brittle and cold.

But like porridge—warm, comforting
and full of natural goodness.

O Lord, grant that we may not like
porridge: stiff, stodgy and hard to stir.

But like cornflakes—crisp, fresh
and ready to serve.

Take your pick!

Barbara Restle

Far North

By Virginia Gest

The mirror lake breathes peace upon the evening air.
I drift in solitary calm.
Dark pines crowd the shore where mist obscures
A noisy family of ducks about to settle for the night.
The sun is gone.
Silently a fish pricks the perfect plane of water.
Circles widen. Blue deepens to purple.
In the day's last light an otter pushes a wedge
of ripples to the farthest shore.
His rhythmic wake subsides.
The first breeze of night brings a lonely chill
From the opaque depths beneath, teeming with silent movement.
In the vastness of the skies above, a few timid stars
Announce the mysterious equilibrium of night.
✻

Camping Out

By Virginia Gest

The moon, a pale disk, hung heavy
In a sky of old pewter.
Fog smothered all brightness
And wrapped a hoary whiteness
In, around, and over the shore.
Tree forms loomed animate, then vanished.
Bat wings swooped downward and were gone.
Throbbing on their cold wet stones,
The frogs kept the pulse of the night.

✳

Barbara Restle

Two Black Cats

By Virginia Gest

Two black cats of graceful elegance live at my
house.
Silent black paws, crisp pointed ears,
Whiskers and fur shining black.
Black as licorice or coal, save for pale green
eyes,
Pink tongue, and a brush-stroke of white at
the throat.
Fat Cat of the ruffled jowls
Pads around with masculine assurance
And easy affability. His sister, Little Cat,
Once frightened by his sallies,
Now plays the role of cleverness.
With satanic conceit they parade through
their realm,
Tails on high like undulating question
marks.
On frosty mornings they rush inside
Like two matched circus prancers
And curl up by the heating vent.
With paws tucked in on all sides and
Eyes blinking sleepily, they are

Two round islands of composure.
That's when they purr, throat and deep
An odd mechanism to sound from such
softness.
The smell of bacon draws them to the
kitchen.
They press their furry backs against my legs.
Wherever I step, the floor seems full of cats.
They eat daintily, watchfully
Crouched on the edge of the paper.
Then the ritual of washing begins.
One takes his cue from the other:
First the paws, then the whiskers and face—
Eyes closed to slits—
Then the head bobs down and down again
As the pink tongue licks the chest shiny
damp.
With a delicate sigh they collapse in double
sprawl,
As limp as a fur neckpiece dropped carelessly.

BIOGRAPHIES MEADOWOOD
RESIDENTS

ELISABETH (BETTY) P. MYERS BAIN

Betty graduated from East Grand Rapids High School in Michigan and earned her B.A. at Vassar College in New York followed by post-graduate studies at Northwestern University. By the time Betty was ten years old she had become a published writer. During her professional career she published verses, crossword puzzles and articles in women's magazines. She wrote textbooks for Scott Foresman and Harper and Rowe. Betty's first book, KATHARYNE LEE BATES, composer of America the Beautiful was published in 1961, followed by twenty-one more non-fiction books. Betty also published many travel articles in the Chicago Tribune as she toured 96 and the worlds 197 independent countries. For 20 years Betty also volunteered at the Bloomington Hospital and 14 years as a docent at the Indiana University Art Museum.

WILLIAM "BILL" BALDWIN

Bill earned his B.S. and Optometry Degrees from Pacific University. After two years of private practice in Indianapolis, he and his family moved to Bloomington in 1953. He earned his Masters and Ph.D. degrees from Indiana University and joined the optometry faculty. In 1963 he returned to Pacific University as Dean of the Pacific University Optometry School. He was President of the New England College of Optometry from 1969 to 1979 and Dean of the University of Houston School of Optometry from 1979 to 1990. During this time he helped organize and serve as President of the River Blindness Foundation. Bill retired in 1999.

OLIMPIA BARBERA

Olimpia was born in Cordoba, Argentina and graduated with Honors from the Provincial University of Cordoba with a major in piano. During her early career she performed with chamber music orchestras in Argentina and Brazil. Olimpia has been actively involved in supporting music education all her life and established a free school of music for under-privileged children in Argentina. President Raul Leoni awarded Olimpia a medal as WOMAN OF THE YEAR in Venezuela after she formed and conducted an orchestra for the deaf and also another one for the blind. In 1992 the Anthony and Olimpia Barbera Music Scholarship was established at the Indiana School of Music.

ROBERT "BOB" F. BLAKELY

Bob is a geophysicist, a scientist who studied the physical properties of rocks. He retired in 1986 after a career of 37 years as a senior scientist with the Indiana Geological Survey and a Professor of Indiana University's Department of Geologic Sciences, where he taught meteorology, geophysics and computing technology.

ROBERT CONRAD BAYER

Bob graduated from Northside High School, Fort Wayne, IN and earned his B.S. degree from Ball State, IN. In 1945 Bob joined the U.S. Maritime and was stationed in Japan in 1946. After his service in WWII he worked for ITT Federal as Project Manager. Later he worked for Cummins Engine Co. as their Washington Representative. His next employment included Eastern Regional Sales Manager for AMBAC, United Technologies and lastly International Sales Manager for Automotive Division.

AL BOISSEVAIN

Al received his bachelor's degree from Middlebury College in Vermont. He earned an aeronautical engineering degree from MIT, worked for NASA in California until his retirement in 1980. He began a second career growing grapes on five acres of vineyard in the foothills of the Sierra Mountains. After four years, Al retired a second time and he realized that he had not read a book in 20 years. His daughter suggested he move to Meadowood Retirement Community and became busy volunteering with Meals on Wheels and found he still has not read that first book.

JOHN P. BROGNEAUX

John graduated from Upland High School in Indiana, earned his B.S. from Ball State in 1932, his Masters degree from Indiana University in 1937 and his Ph.D. in Physical Education and Health in 1947. During WWII John served for three years of active duty in the American-European and Pacific Theater and for 17 years was in the Navy Reserve. John coached basketball in several Indiana high schools, including 18 years as coach in Bloomington High School. For 17 years he worked in Indiana University in the School of Education and H.P.E.R. He received the Ball State Athletic Hall of Fame.

LIBBY BUCK

Libby earned a B.A. in 1946 from the University of Minnesota and a M.S. in 1956 from Duke University in Counseling. For several years Libby and husband Professor Roger Buck lived in Oxford, England and later in Ghana where he taught philosophy. Libby was on the Committee of Ministry and Counsel of the Society of Friends, (Quaker) which has pastoral duties. Libby was one of the founding members of NEW LEAF, NEW LIFE FOR JAIL IMPROVEMENT.

ELEANOR BYRNES

Eleanor graduated from the University of Massachusetts in Amherst before entering Indiana University in the graduate program of Russian Languages. Her husband, Professor of European History and their seven children lived on various campuses before settling in Bloomington where Eleanor has been active as a volunteer in the Red Cross and the Bloomington Hospital. She and her husband traveled extensively in Russia.

ERNEST "CAM" E. CAMPAIGNE

Ernest earned his B.S. from Northwest University in 1936, Masters Degree in 1938 and his Ph.D. in 1940. Ernest came to Indiana University in the Army Special Training Program in 1943. He worked at Oak Ridge National Laboratories until 1955. He left for a Sabbatical leave at Cambridge University in England in 1964. Later he accepted a Fulbright Scholarship in Australia. He worked for Dow Chemical until 1980. After working in Spain and Germany he returned to Indiana and in 1988. He represented the United States on the International Board of Pure and Applied Chemistry.

CAROLYN CARLISLE

Carolyn graduated from Palo Alto High School in California, and graduated from the College of the Pacific. She was also trained in a San Francisco school as a fashion model. Carolyn was a student of classical music and piano.

LEDFORD CARTER

Professor Carter is retired from Indiana University where he taught courses in educational motion picture production and writing for educational media. He is retired from the U.S. Army as Lieutenant Colonel after serving in Field Artillery, Civil Affairs and Intelligence Branch. Ledford came to Bloomington in 1951 from Athens, Georgia where he had been the managing director of The Southern Educational Education Film Service, a cooperative that served nine southeastern states and Tennessee Valley Authority. Ledford and his wife Julia have lived in Meadowood for 29 years. In 2005 Ledford founded the MEADOWOOD ANTHOLOGY and formed the first committee with Ginnie Guest and Barbara Restle.

VIOLET FUNK CHIAPPETTA

Violet trained at Huntington College and Ball State as a teacher and librarian. She served in several Indiana high schools and later in Lima, Peru. During WWII she was technical librarian in the Women's Auxiliary Army Cops, and later at the University of Michigan. After marrying Professor Michael Chiappetta, they lived in various states and countries including Latin America and Hangzhou University in China.

BERNARD "BERNIE" CLAYTON JR.

After Bernie attended Indiana University he worked as a reporter for the Indianapolis Star. In 1940 he joined the news staff of Life Magazine in New York City. When the United States entered WWII Bernie was assigned the job of Bureau Chief by Life Magazine in San Francisco. As the war progressed, Life Magazine opened an office in Hawaii, one in the Philippines and lastly one in Japan. Bernie acted as bureau chief in each country. After the war ended, Bernie was employed as public relations director for two companies in San Francisco. Taking one year off from business enterprises he began his career as a free-lance reporter and photographer. In 1966 Indiana University invited Bernie to work in university relations which led him and his wife Marjorie to make Bloomington their home. During these years, Bernie turned to his talent as a cook. Simon and Schuster published Bernie's six cook books with recipes for breads, pastries, soups and stews.

BILL CHRISTIANSEN

Bill graduated from Drake University in Des Moines, Iowa in 1947. He worked for 20 years in the advertising department of Marshall Field land then worked for Philips Electronics in Evanston, Illinois. In 1984 he retired and moved to Bloomington, IN.

IRVING DANIELSON

Irving received a bachelor's degree with high honors in chemical engineering from the University of Minnesota which led to a successful career in business with assignments in Europe, becoming a Director for Stewart-Warner Corporation.

LUISE DAVID

Luise was born in Bavaria. She immigrated with her infant son to America as the Nazi regime began to target the Jewish citizens. Within a year her husband also emigrated. Luise worked as a claims adjuster in the New York City's garment district. She is the author of HOW WE SURVIVED.

EDGAR deJEAN

Edgar received his D.D.S. and M.S.D. degrees from Indiana University School of Dentistry. He served in the US Army Dental Corps from 1944 to 1947. After discharge from the Army he practiced general dentistry in Salem, IN until 1958. After residencies at the University of Louisville School of Dentistry in 1962, Edgar received his award of Diplomate American Board of Oral Surgery. Between 1962 and 1988 he was part-time faculty at the University of Louisville School of Dentistry. He retired in 1994. Edgar was active in his community; was elected County Councilman and also was a member of school boards and held several positions in his church. Edgar is well known for his professional showmanship in impersonating Mark Twain.

ELIZABETH DROEGE

Elizabeth has been going to school, off and on, for most of her life. She attended Northwestern University at the Chicago College campus for three years while working for United Airlines. It was a great combination of school and adventure, and the people at Northwestern were tolerant of her rather frequent absences from class.

ALFRED "FREDDY" DIAMANT

In 1939, after Kristalnacht and the rise of Nazism, Freddy escaped from Vienna, his birthplace and found sanctuary in Kitchener

Refugee Camp in England. In 1940 Freddy immigrated to the United States. Within one month after Pearl Harbor he knew he had a personal stake in the coming war and reported for induction into the U.S. Army at Fort Devens, Massachusetts. In 1944, after his training with the Military Intelligence Service, Freddy was transferred to England and earned his parachute wings. Of the eighteen men parachuting into Normandy on D-Day thirteen were killed and four taken prisoners. The German soldier who took Freddy prisoner shot him. He was treated in a German field hospital and later in hospitals in England. The bullet lodged too close to his spine and was never removed. Freddy earned his B.A. in 1947 and his M.A. in 1948 from Indiana University and his Ph.D. from Yale in 1957. He taught at the University of Florida, at Haverford College and Indiana University. He retired from IU in 1988. During his academic career he was a visiting professor in various universities in the United States and in Europe. He was granted a Fulbright Scholarship and awarded a Guggenheim Fellowship and an E-xcellence in Teaching Award in 1975 and also in 1985.

ELLA WADE FOX

Ella is a native of Howe, Indiana, and a graduate of the University of Michigan with a B.A. degree in Education. During WWII Ella applied to the American Red Cross and was assigned over-seas duty. After 42 days on a troop ship carrying 5,000 troops and 30 women the ship landed in Calcutta. No one knew where they were headed until reaching the Panama Canal. Ella worked as a Red Cross Staff Assistant in Karachi and also an Army rest camp in the Himalayas where she met Army Officer John Fox, her future husband.

JOHN W. FOX

John graduated from Indiana University School of Business in 1941. He was in the U.S. Army Air Corps for five years including service in Burma and India where he and Ella found each other. He was in the advertising agency business in Manhattan for 20 years, then the executive recruiting business in New York and Chicago where he and a partner had their own firm for 11 years locating senior-level people for corporations. He retired to Beaufort, S.C. and eventually moved to Bloomington, IN.

MARY FIELDING

Mary and her husband Gale lived in Stockland Township, Il. for 68 years until moving to Meadowood Retirement Community. Although she had taken short courses in art at the University of Illinois, she had no formal art training. She has worked in many artistic media including ceramics. Her drawings have been published in three books: PRAIRIE SKYSCRAPERS, MILFORD NOW AND THEN, and also MORE MILFORD.

ESTHER FEINBERG GABER

Esther graduated from Chareroi High School in Pennsylvania and attended University of Pittsburgh. She worked as a business sales representative and in public relations. Esther's volunteer activities include Planned Parenthood, Meals on Wheels and visiting nurse care.

HOWARD GEST

Howard is Distinguished Professor Emeritus of Microbiology and Adjunct Professor of History and Philosophy of Science at Indiana University. As a chemist on the Manhattan Project in Oak Ridge, he did basic research on the radioactive elements formed in uranium fission. Later he taught at Western Reserve Medical School and Washington University of St. Louis. Howard has been a visiting research scholar at California Tech, Stanford University, and Oxford University. He was awarded a Guggenheim fellowship twice and has served on various government committees. Howard is a Fellow of the American Academy of Arts and Science. He has published more than 300 technical papers and essays. He enjoys classical music and opera. In 1998 he married Virginia Ollis.

VIRGINIA "GINNY" GEST

Virginia came from a stable home in Scranton, PA, the youngest of three children. Her father, a regional bank auditor, provided for a comfortable home: piano lessons, summers at the lake, and community activities. Church and Scouting shaped her life, and her first husband was a university pastor at Indiana University. She had excellent teachers in high school and college, with a strong interest in art and literature. After raising three children, she graduated from IU in 1982, majoring in English. Virginia's adult interests are focused on building peace and justice, keeping in touch with an extended family. Ginnie was instrumental in the production of the quarterly MEADOWOOD ANTHOLOGY.

LEONARD H.D. GORDON

In 1953 Leonard earned his Master of Arts Degree at Indiana University in Chinese History and Languages. He entered military service and studied Chinese Mandarin in the U.S. Army Language School of Monterey, CA and served in Army Intelligence in Tokyo,

Japan. He earned his Ph.D. in Modern Chinese History at the University of Michigan followed by a Fulbright Scholarship. Leonard served in the U.S. Department of State from 1961 to 1963 in Washington, D.C. He then accepted an appointment at the University of Wisconsin and later at Purdue University and became Chairman of Asian Studies.

BETH VAN VORST GRAY

Beth was born in Harvey, Illinois and her husband, Ralph D. Gray Professor Emeritus of History, Indiana University Purdue are both published writers. Beth established a business career in Indianapolis. Beth is a member of the Meadowood Anthology Committee and is now project manager.

HENRY H. GRAY

Henry received the B.S. degree from Haverford College in 1943, the M.S. degree from the University of Michigan in 1946 and the Ph.D. degree from The Ohio State University in 1954. He then moved to Bloomington, IN and began a 33 year career with the Indiana Geological Survey as Coal Geologist, Map Editor, and Head Stratigrapher. He currently is a Research Affiliate with that organization, where he continues studies in the geology of Indiana. In 1992 he shared the John C. Frye award in Environmental Geology, and in 1998 the Professional Geologists of Indiana granted him their Distinguished Service Award.

PATRICIA "PAT" HASSID

After Pat trained as a nurse in Boston, she earned her master's degree in education. During the time her husband Roger went to medical school Pat helped to support

him working as a nurse. Pat has had a long-time interest in pain reduction during childbirth through psychological and physical preparation during pregnancy. Pat is the award-winning author of the book "TEXTBOOK FOR CHILDBIRTH EDUCATORS", and also directed teacher training for educators for many years.

JEAN SINCLAIR HERRMANN

Jean graduated from Bloomington High School South in 1937 and earned her B.A. in Sociology from Indiana University in 1941. Jean trained at the National Girl Scout Training Camp Edith Macy in Wisconsin. For three years Jean worked as a Girl Scout Director in Kenosha, WI. In 1943 Jean married Joyce Rockwell Herrmann after he earned his Law Degree from Northwestern Law School. As the wife of a U.S. State Department employee in the Foreign Service, the couple with their five children and traveled and lived in many countries, including Pakistan, Poland, India, Lebanon, Jerusalem, Jordan and Greece. After living in Bethesda, Maryland for 21 years, the couple retired to Bloomington, IN.

THEA HOSEK

Thea and her husband and their children lived in Peru, Indiana where Thea was active in several community organizations including United Way, Chamber of Commerce and Big Brothers and Big Sisters. During this time, Thea was named Woman of the Year and later was named Citizen of the Year. Thea's husband Robert was in the U.S. Air Force for 25 years.

JULIE KING

Julie and her husband Jack divide their time between Meadowood and their home in Northern Wisconsin near Lake Superior. In Bloomington they serve on "Earth Stewards" at First Presbyterian Church.

ROSETTA S. SOLARI KNOX

Rosetta's early childhood was in northern Italy. Her high school years were in Scotland at Montrose Academy. She earned her Ph.D. in Venice at Ca'Foscari University in Italy. Rosetta taught Italian at the Berlitz School of Languages in Pittsburg, Pennsylvania and also taught French and Italian at the University of Louisville in Kentucky. Early in her life Rosetta was active in the Resistance movement in northern Italy during WWII after Mussolini was killed and the country occupied by the Germany Army. For a short time Rosetta was imprisoned by the Germans.

ELAINE LETHEM

Elaine earned her B.S. degree in 1945 at Kansas State University and her Masters degree in Sociology at the University of Illinois in 1970 and then entered doctoral studies. Elaine worked as a Therapeutic Dietitian at the Children's Hospital in Cook County, Chicago and later as Assistant Director of Food Services at University of Missouri in Kansas City. Elaine also worked as Instructor of Sociology at Harper College in Palestine, Ill.

RICHARD (Dick) LETSINGER

During WWII Richard served in the U.S. Army in the European Theater. He was assigned as assistant to the British Brigadier General in London and later in France and Germany. After his discharge he enrolled at Indiana University and graduated with a Bachelor of Arts in History. After graduation, Richard worked for 40 years in the real estate business in Bloomington.

TERRY LOUCKS

Terry was a physics professor at Iowa State University and became the Chief Scientist at Rockwell International. He started a company that made chromatographic instruments for the pharmaceutical industry. When he sold that business, he went sailing in the Caribbean for several years. After he sold his sailboat he made Meadowood Retirement Community his home.

ROBERT RODMAN LUDLOW

Robert earned his B.S. degree from Purdue in 1949, his Masters of Business Administration in 1973 and his Ph.D. in Applied Economics from Purdue in 1979. He worked for 22 years in the retail business as owner of the Ludlow Modern Furniture Company in Indianapolis from 1949 to 1972. After retirement, Robert volunteered his services as consultant with SCORE from 1993 to 2002.

ALEXANDRIA (SANDY) M. LYNCH

Sandy received her B.A. in English with Honors at Oberlin College and her Master's in Education at Indiana University. She worked in publishing in New York City, and returned to Indiana to become editor of an employee newsletter at Bloomington's RCA Television Plant and also worked there in Human Resources. She subsequently became Training Specialist at Ford Electronics in

Bedford, IN and also produced a weekly employee newsletter for 23 years. She worked as Director of the SOAR! Adult Literacy Program in Lawrence County, and as Editor at Option Six, a producer of online corporate training courses. At this time Sandy works at Indiana University as Writer/Photographer in the Physical Plant, producing a quarterly new magazine. Sandy has been on the staff of MEADOWOOD ANTHOLOGY as Production Editor since 2006.

EUGENE A. MERRELL

Lieutenant Colonel Eugene Merrell retired from the U.S. Air Force in 1978 after six years in the Reserves and 30 years on active duty. He was a Command Pilot of flying status for 31 years. He served four tours in the Philippines, Korea, and Vietnam. He was awarded the Bronze Star and Air Medal. He was assigned to Indiana University as Professor of Aerospace Studies, then to the "elite" 1st Air Transport Squadron at Andrews Air Force Base. After he retired from the Kincheloe AFB in Michigan, he settled in Bloomington and in 2005 moved to Meadowood Retirement Community.

JUNE MILLER

As a child in Hollywood June had several small movie parts as an actress and tap dancer. Her show business experience prepared her later in life for a career in radio and TV in Toledo and also Indianapolis where June anchored the TV show called THE NOON REPORT. She graduated from Indiana University with a Bachelor of Arts degree. June was popular as an inspirational speaker in Indiana. Later in life, June worked in the real estate business in Bloomington.

LOIS MORRIS

Lois was born in Lebanon, Indiana. Lois was employed at the New Jersey Correctional Institution for Women from 1946 to 1976. When Lois retired she held the position as Assistant Superintendent. She attended Purdue and Rutgers Universities. In 1978, she became a volunteer with the Pinelands Preservation Alliance leading nature and bus trips into the New Jersey pine lands. While there she won many environmental awards. Lois moved to Meadowood in 2004 and pioneered the bluebird box monitoring program.

NAOMI OSBORNE

Naomi was an alumna of Indiana University. During her professional career with the United Nations, she worked in Gaza, the Congo and the Philippines. She was director of university relations at Indiana University East.

DAN FRANK OSEN

Dan graduated from Anita Public High School in Iowa and from Drake University in Des Moines, Iowa, and in 1952 graduated with a B.S. degree in Pharmacy. The next two years Dan served in the U.S. Army as a pharmacist in Fort Sill, Oklahoma. For one year he worked in a drug store as pharmacist in Lawton, OK before accepting employment by Eli Lilly and Company in Indianapolis. He continued to work for Eli Lilly for 34 years retiring in 1988. His first job description was as a raw materials procurement employee followed by his being in charge of scheduling biological production. In 1960 he was appointed chief of government bids and contracts. Dan's love of music, both for piano

Barbara Restle

and voice, began when he was very young. Dan plays classical and popular music by ear and by note. Dan and his wife Voncile, sang with the Indianapolis Symphonic Choir. Through the years, the couple sang with this choir performing in the Kennedy Center for the Performing Arts in Washington, D.C. and also at Carnegie Hall in New York City.

NORMAN VANCE OVERLY

Norman earned his B.S. in English and Elementary Education and his Masters Degree from Kent State University. He entered a Special Study in Theology and Missions at Berkeley Baptist Divinity School and earned a Ph.D. in Curriculum and History and Comparative Education from Ohio State University. He taught Junior High School and Junior College English in Kanto Kaguin, Yokohama, Japan. Including Missionary service, Norman and his wife Jeanne lived in Japan for six years. He was Assistant Professor of Education at Becknell University, and Associate Secretary for Supervision and Curriculum Development and Professor of Education at Indiana University. His service in the Army included his award of "1st" Army Corps Soldier of the Month.

NEVIN RABER

Nevin is a native Hoosier, was a Major in the U.S. Army, graduated from Purdue with a B.S. degree and from Indiana University with M.A. degree in History and another M.A. in Library Science. In his younger years he worked as a railroad telegrapher. He was a librarian at Indiana University School of Business and acted as consultant with the library's design and operation. He is an Indiana University Business School Librarian Emeritus.

OSWARLD GLEASON "OZZY" RAGATZ

Indian University Professor Emeritus of Music, came to IU in 1942 as instructor of Organ and Theory. Over the ensuing years, the IU Organ Department, with a faculty of four, grew to include as many as fifty-five organ majors, both undergraduate and graduate students. When he retired after forty-one years as Chairman of the Organ Department at IU, more than seventy of his graduates held teaching posts in institutions of higher learning.

As a concert artist he was heard in nearly every state in the Union as well as in Europe and the Far East. He held posts as organist-choirmaster in Rochester and Scarsdale, New York, also for ten years in Bloomington, IN at the First Methodist Church and twenty-five years at First Presbyterian Church.

BARBARA BLACKLEDGE RESTLE

Barbara was born in Paris of American parents and was brought up in Vienna until WWII. While working as an x-ray technician in NYC she attended Columbia University and New School of Social Research and later earned her B.A. degree from Indiana University Ernie Pyle School of Journalism. She was President of the Sassafras Audubon Society in the 1970's. Barbara owned and managed farms in Mississippi and Indiana. Most of her 200 acre farm in northwestern Monroe County is now part of a 600 acre wetlands refuge. She served in the Peace Corps in the South Pacific consulting farmers on a 3,000 acre cattle scheme funded by the World Bank. In 2005 Barbara and Ledford Carter published the first quarterly magazine, the MEADOWOOD ANTHOLOGY.

JOSEPH "JOE" REZITS

In 1948 Joe was awarded a scholarship at the Curtis Institute of Music, studied piano with Isabelle Vengerova, and was awarded his Artist Diploma. At the age of 23, Joe made his North American debut with Eugene Ormandy and the Philadelphia Orchestra as winner of the Philadelphia Orchestra Youth Auditions. Joe received his Bachelor of Music in 1954 and Master of Music in 1955 from the University of Illinois, his Teachers College Professional Diploma in 1964 from Columbia University, and his Doctor of Musical Arts in 1973 from the University of Colorado. In 1971 Joe was named Professor of Music at Indiana University; however, his IU career began in 1957 when appointed Assistant Professor. Through the years Joe has been visiting Professor for conservatories and universities in Australia, China, Japan, Singapore, Malaysia and institutions in the United States and Canada.

CHARLES A. (CHUCK) ROCKWOOD

Chuck graduated from Indiana University and the U.S. Army Command General Staff College. His Army career spanned 20 years. During WWII he was stationed in Europe. After the war he was stationed in Panama, Thailand, Vietnam and the United States. After discharge from the Army he worked on the staff of Indiana University Administration.

DOLORES (DEE) ROCKWOOD

Dee graduated from Huntington High School in West Virginia and graduated with a B.A, from Central Connecticut College in 1953. After earning her teaching license in 1973 Dee taught in Bloomington's elementary schools and also earned her Master's degree in Education from Indiana University in 1979. During her high school and college years, Dee pursued her love of art in watercolor and also practicing old English lettering. Dee and her husband, "Chuck" are parents to a combined family of eight children, 14 grandchildren and multiple great-grandchildren.

ELISABETH M. SAVICH

Elisabeth earned her degree in Home Economics from Carnegie Mellon University and was trained as a dietician and in homeopathy. In the 1960's she was active in politics. For many years Elisabeth volunteered in the NC Crisis Line and in the Bloomington area volunteered in several shelters serving food to the needy.

MIRIAM ROSENZWEIG

Miriam spent the first twelve years of her life in Munich and Vienna. After Germany annexed Austria in 1938, her family fled the Nazi regime and settled in New York, where she went to high school. She earned a bachelor's degree from Cornell University. After her marriage to Norbert Rosenzweig, a physicist, they moved to Chicago, where she worked in several medical research laboratories, occasionally interrupted by the birth and nurture of their three children. Her husband died in the 1970's, and she moved to Bloomington, IN. At that time she decided to change professions. She took courses at the Indiana University School of Journalism, then began working for the Indiana Alumni Magazine. She worked as the Magazine's associate editor for 12 years.

ROBIN BLACK-SCHAFFER

Robin was an emergency room physician and a professor in Indiana University Bloomington's Medical Sciences Department. Her husband was Professor Bernard Black-Schaffer Emeritus of Pathology at Indiana University.

NANCY SEWARD TAYLOR

Nancy, whose youthful portrait adorns a wall of the Brown County Playhouse, pursued a successful and professional stage career. She also worked as a communications disorder therapist. Nancy is a Bloomington native whose great, great grandfather constructed the wind vane fish above the Monroe County Court House. Her ancestors settled in Bloomington in 1821.

WALTER FULLER TAYLOR

In 1964 Walter received his Ph.D. in American Literature at Emory University. He was a professor at Georgia Tech. and also taught at LSU, Hawaii, and Rhode Island. He was awarded Professor Emeritus at the University of Texas at El Paso. In 1983 Illinois Press published his book, FAULKNER'S SEARCH FOR THE SOUTH. In 2005 Walter published a book of mystery, A TICKET TO SOMEWHERE.

BOB WEBB

Bob was born in Kokomo, Indiana. His first two years of college were at the Indiana University Regional Campus in Kokomo and his junior year at the Bloomington campus. In his senior year he studied Radiological Health at the IU Medical Center in Indianapolis, studying the effects of radiation on the human body. He graduated in 1952 with a B.S. degree. Bob was a graduate student at Taft Engineering Center in Cincinnati, Ohio. During the 1970's he developed procedures to ship low level radioactive waste as well as hazardous chemicals.

JAMES "JIM" E. WEIGAND

In 1952 Jim earned his B.A. from Augustana College. He earned his Masters Degree in Education from Northern Illinois University and in 1964 his Ed.D. from Indiana University. He remained at IU as Professor of Science of Education. During his academic career he held the position of Assistant to President John Ryan and later became Dean of the School of Continuing Studies. After Jim retired in 1993 the President of IU Foundation Kurt Simic invited Jim to join him at the IU Foundation offering him a private office with secretary. Jim accepted this position and is at this time is still working at the IU Foundation. In 2006 Jim was selected "Distinguished Alumni" of Indiana University for his 46 years as an administrator and faculty member.